TALISMAN

With Best Wishes
By
[signature]
(N. ELANSEZHIAN)

TALISMAN

Extreme Emotions of Dalit Liberation

THIRUMAAVALAVAN

Translated from the Tamil by
MEENA KANDASAMY

Introduction by
GAIL OMVEDT

Illustrations by
VEERA SANTHANAM

Samya

TALISMAN: EXTREME EMOTIONS OF DALIT LIBERATION
was first published on 6 December 2003 by Samya, an imprint
of Bhatkal and Sen, 16 Southern Avenue, Kolkata 700 026

© 2003 Thol. Thirumaavalavan and Meena Kandasamy

ISBN 81-85604-68-1

All rights reserved. No part of this book
may be reproduced or utilized in any form or by
any means without prior written permission from the publisher.

Front cover photograph: aerial view of Thirumaavalavan addressing a Viduthalai Chiruthaigal meeting of 12 August 2002 at Tiruchi to condemn the Thinniyam atrocity (where caste-fanatics had forced two Dalits to eat human excrement).

Back cover photograph: Thirumaavalavan delivers his speech on revolutionary Ambedkar's birth anniversary, 14 April 2003, at the Viduthalai Chiruthaigal meeting in Madurai, where more than 10,800 people took Tamil names.

Distributed by Popular Prakashan
Mumbai, Delhi, Kolkata

Layout and design by Meena Kandasamy and printed by Swapna Printing,
52 Raja Rammohan Roy Sarani, Kolkata 700 009

Published by Mandira Sen for SAMYA
an imprint of Bhatkal and Sen,
16 Southern Avenue, Kolkata 700 026

*an explosive talisman
to fuel the fire of revolution*

c.o.n.t.e.n.t.s

Preface
    Even the Writings Stink of Casteism   ix

Acknowledgements   xiii

Introduction
    Thunder Out of the Cheri by Gail Omvedt   xiv

Transaltor's Note
    Che Guevara of the Cheris by Meena Kandasamy   xxv

1. What Rules the Nation: Law or Casteism?   1
2. Dalit Uprising: Will It Put an End to Dravidian Politics?   15
3. Will America Drop Global 'Supercop'ism?   19
4. Rule of Caste Is the Rule of India!   23
5. Is Democracy a Diya or Daylight?   33
6. First We Will Prevent the Terrorism of Law!   39
7. Castration of History   43
8. Police Terrorism   47
9. Kannagi: A Symbol of Militancy   59
10. Are You the Gandhian Monkeys?   63
11. A Slap in the Face!   69
12. Judgments: Not to Be Corrected, but to Be Changed   75
13. Democracy Is the Religion! Humanism Is the Veda!   81
14. Dreams-Imaginations-Papers   85
15. Majority Only for Democracy and Equality   89

Contents

16. Politics in Tamil Nadu: Reeling Around Cinema — 93
17. The Real Faces of the Dravidian Parties — 97
18. Legislative Assembly: Not for the Last — 101
19. His Excellency: Needed Again — 105
20. No Need for the Election Commission! — 109
21. Party Colours on the Bull's Horn: The President's Election — 115
22. 'They' Are Superior to Humans — 119
23. Eelam Is the Foetus of the Tigers — 123
24. Somalia in Tamil Nadu? — 127
25. A Raw Tamilian Is Needed! — 131
26. Musharraf Is Also an Indian! — 135
27. Even a Private Government Can Be Formed! — 139
28. Why Was the Mark of Vishnu Thrust? — 143
29. Tamil Rule Bloomed in the Vanni Forest! — 147
30. ADMK Is Not a Periyar Movement, It Is a Periyavaal Movement — 151
31. Change of Name: Not Just a Retrieval of Language, but of History — 157
32. Are Saivism and Vaishnavism Hindu Religions? — 165
33. Must Venmani Be Fenced? — 169
34. Is the Tamil Land Infertile and Fallow? — 175

Index — 179

p.r.e.f.a.c.e

EVEN THE WRITINGS STINK OF CASTEISM!

Here, there are many writers who milk money by writing pages and pages on what happens in semi-darkness in dilapidated buildings and in derelict vehicles; with their prying eyes they probe and grope, widely and deeply, and dig out to expose the weaknesses of sexual desires of the lay or ordinary people on the roadside.

Here, there are many writers with a regressive mindset, who instead of approaching and analysing the reason for such lives, taking into account the background of political, social and economic exploitation, do not wish to reveal this background even if they have understood it. They vulgarize the lay people, betray them to the dominant ruling gangs, push and force them into the degraded and last position.

Here, there are many, many things that have not been recorded or come into view of such writers.

The sons-of-the-soil, who lived in the centre of the Chennai metropolis supposedly 'pollute' the beauty and cleanliness of Chennai; so they have been driven away thirty kilometres from the city. Because of this cruelty, these people are deprived of the handful of land that they own, their families are scattered, they lose their identity; yet, their plight of suffering never comes into the view of such writers. Even if they see it, they don't get angry or feel ashamed about it.

Today, a gang that covers up the historical background of the oppression that has been systematically imposed for ages and ages in the name of caste, in the name of religion, by the supremacist ruling class in collusion with the governing authorities, that continuously concocts and blacks out history, has encroached on the literary world. Such a gang, even while riding through a *cheri* (in Tamil, a Dalit ghetto) or a slum, hold their noses and scornfully twist their faces. In the Chennai metropolis alone, approximately ten lakh people live in *poromboke* land, hunched in their huts, without any title deed. There too, they live amidst the gut-wrenching smell of the Cooum River's banks, alongside gutters and sewers, in roadside lanes and nooks and crannies, like pigs and like dogs, they exist and wander in disgrace. Did these people choose this disgraceful life of their own accord? What is the background for their plight? Today who is there in the literary world to worry or express sympathy about this?

At no point of time have writers, litterateurs, religious heads, heads of mutts, political leaders, professionals and other experts belonging to such categories, bothered about or condemned the appalling atrocities and the oppression by the power-crazy that takes place in the name of caste!

A casteist mob brutally lynched five Dalits in Duleena in Jhajjar district in Haryana, because the Dalits had skinned a dead cow. The purity of the cow had been spoilt! The caste-crazy gang had become angry only because 'even if it was dead, can a cow be skinned?' So it seems, that for the sake of a dead cow, five Dalits can be murdered! The 'guru of this whole Jagat [world]', the Kanchi Sankaracharya himself justifies this! No eminent person in India has come forward to condemn this cruelty, this disgrace.

For the sole reason of their being people of the cheri, Dalits have excrement and urine forced into their mouths; such cruelties take place in broad daylight without the least bit of reserve. Recently, in the Madurai district, a woman poured excrement mixed in water on the face of Muthumari, a Dalit woman of the Keela Urappanur village, in front of several others. The woman who did this was an 'upper' caste woman! How can a person be a writer, if she/he doesn't surge with emotions even after she/he sees and hears about such atrocities?

On 15 August 2003, India's Independence Day, a Dalit Panchayat President Duraiarasu of Sottathatti in the Sivaganga district was beaten with a slipper by a caste-fanatic who questioned, *Oru palla paiya eppadi desiya kodi ettralam?* (lit. How can a Pallar man hoist the National Flag?) There are countless casteist atrocities like this! But there was no sign of rage or uproar from any corner of the literary world? In this land, even the writings stink of casteism! A caste-fanatic frenzy that prevents Dalits from even filing nomination papers in the reserved Panchayat constituencies of Pappapatti, Keeripatti, Nattarmangalam and Kottakatchiyendal has been publicly on the rampage for the past seven years. This is against law and democracy. This is a challenge imposed by the casteists! But the entire Tamil Nadu state and the Indian subcontinent are silent. With the exception of the singular voice of the Viduthalai Chiruthaigal that roars from the cheri, there has been not any whimper or whisper from any other place.

If silence looms in the political world on the basis of political benefit, on what basis does this terseness exist in the literary world?

For how many more generations will such oppression and subjugation that have been permeated for countless generations continue? All through this land, there is a deluge of chronicles of bloodstains because of the frenzied communalist dances of destruction in those days of monarchy, when the rule of the state was associated with religion. But even half a century after the flowering of a secular government was announced, casteist and communalist riots have not stopped. Equality, democracy, humanism have all become objects of ridicule!

Even historical evidence and testimonies of the completely merciless, cruel and atrocious extermination that was unleashed to annihilate Buddhism and Jainism have been deviously destroyed. Such historical records have been destroyed only because the history of the oppressed people is continuously blacked out; for thousands of years one-quarter of the people in the vast expanse of Indian territory languish and are trapped in the prison of the cheri without being able to regain freedom.

It is a blatant and visible truth that the literary world does not express the necessary concern about this. In this context, the Viduthalai Chiruthaigal, which organizes the oppressed people living in the cheri and crusades towards annihilation of caste, is concerned about the documentation of atrocities and the people's retaliation against atrocities. As a result of such a motivation, the Viduthalai Chiruthaigal records it as much as possible in their monthly magazine *Thaaimann* (Motherland).

When historical records and chronicles evolve as writings and literature, they obtain the strength of igniting revolution and uprising by the oppressed masses. So even if it were not possible to mould into literature the volcano of surging thoughts and emotions, the idea of pouring it all as words came to me.

The *India Today* Tamil weekly magazine gave the opportunity as an outlet and a channel to unburden that eagerness and influence. The wonderful opportunity to write once in a fortnight, twice a month for three years (2001, 2002, 2003) was given. In that manner, for thirty-four weeks, the stormy emotions and thoughts of turmoil that burst out about the contemporary issues were structured and compiled as writings under various heads, and it has taken shape as a book today.

This is not a document that once written, stays buried in the dust of libraries or falls into the quagmire of falsity and distortion by the media. This is not a document where there is a parade of a correlation of collected statistics and gathered evidence. On the contrary, this is the explosion of the emotions of liberation that have burst from the depths of the mind of a first or ancient race, repressed as the last people.

THIRUMAAVALAVAN
03 NOV 2003

a.c.k.n.o.w.l.e.d.g.e.m.e.n.t.s

We offer our deep appreciation to Gail Omvedt who wrote the introduction for this volume; indeed, we feel priveleged that in spite of her busy schedule she managed to make time for our book. Our foremost thanks go to Anand Natarajan, former editor of the Tamil weekly *India Today*, for giving the author an opportunity to record his views on the contemporary issues of the day. It is because of his invitation that a leader who works for the oppressed could make a foray into the literary world. In this context, we also thank Ravikumar of Navayana for his encouragement. We also thank the senior subeditors of *India Today*, Sadasivam, Kavitha Muralidharan and Pir Mohammed.

We acknowledge our gratitude to Vanniyarasu, associate editor of *Thaaimann*, who compiled the original Tamil manuscripts of the author that were written for *India Today*. We sincerely thank Kavini, who typed out the Tamil originals and who helped us in the selection of photographs. We also thank Paavarasu, Magizhvarasu, Ambedarasu, Paavalan, Yazhpaanan and Tamilkathir of the Viduthalai Chiruthaigal for their untiring efforts. All the photographs used in this book are copyright of the Thaaimann Trust.

We greatly appreciate and cherish the help and encouragement by K. Amal and Henry Jerome of AICUF, particularly in the documentation. We thank Lakshmi Berwa for his high doses of optimism and James Sundar for his suggestions. Our thanks are due to Sharmila Rege, Ram Puniyani, Neerav Patel and Virendra Ghogare for their encouragement and direly needed suggestions.

We also thank Benita, Kuttirevathy and Sajitha Shankar, who helped us in this production. We thank Mandira Sen and her colleagues at Samya; we were racing against unimaginable deadlines, and they were such a joy to work with. Our thanks are due to S. A. Showrirajan, managing director of Students Xerox and Nagarajan and designer Pughazendi for the cover design. We thank artist Veera Santhanam for his enthusiasm and efforts and Ayesha Sarkar of Kolkata for her help on the cover. Our gratitude also goes to Kandasamy, Vasantha Kandasamy and Kama, for their interest and dedication and all-round help which greatly contri-buted to the making of this book.

i.n.t.r.o.d.u.c.t.i.o.n

THUNDER OUT OF THE CHERI

Dalits are fighting for their human rights in Tamil Nadu today with more violence than in many other parts of India. In a land which knew a powerful movement directed against Brahminism, caste and superstition, it is shocking to read of some of these incidents: of Dalits being forced to eat excrement, massacred by the police, of Dalit Panchayat Presidents being terrorized into giving up their positions, of numerous occasions of Dalits being prevented by force from exercising their voting rights, of police slaughter of striking workers. It is appalling to learn that the mass attacks on Dalits by Thevars in the southern districts started a few years back simply because a bus was named after a Dalit freedom fighter.

But it would be a mistake to see this as simply a matter of atrocities; the atrocities are in part a sign of the fact that Dalits are coming forward in masses and fighting back. Atrocities go unrecorded and unnoticed when slavery is accepted. Today the situation is different. There is an upsurge and a thunder coming out of Tamil Nadu's cheris today and the existence of atrocities is evidence of this very assertion, this fight.

Thirumaavalavan, whose writings are translated here, has been one of the most militant and charismatic leaders of this new Dalit movement in Tamil Nadu, a movement which has fought for equality at all levels, and has included good deal of political experimentation as well as intense intellectual debate. These articles show him as something more, an important intellectual of the movement, taking positions on the issues of women's liberation, Tamil nationalism, economic rights, Indian and Tamil history, oppression and exploitation of Muslim and other minorities, and the future of democracy. Thirumaavalavan is the founder of the Viduthalai Chiruthaigal (Liberation Panthers; the other major Dalit-based party is the Puthiya Tamizhagam led by Dr. Krishnaswamy). He has been influenced by revolutionary Left trends as well as by a wave of Ambedkarite radicalism that swept Tamil Nadu in the early 1990s. In the early years the Viduthalai Chiruthaigal took an anti-parliamentary stand that emphasized fighting back against atrocities and criticized all the Dravidian parties, including the DMK, for turning a radical anti-caste movement into a simple anti-Brahminism that brought upper non-Brahmins to power but did nothing for Dalits. Now the Viduthalai Chiruthaigal is allied with the DMK and hoping to transform that party while maintaining an autonomous political identity of Dalits.

Is this a retreat from revolutionary politics? To say that would be to use a false and superficial definition for 'revolutionary'. Thirumaavalavan's position is in fact a stand more consistent with Ambedkar's own political leadership. Ambedkar had sought to use parliamentary politics, and had vigorously attempted alliances (and sometimes made them) with non-Brahmin political forces even though it was very often non-Brahmins (the OBCs of today) whom Dalits confronted directly in fighting against atrocities at the village level. Vasant Moon's story of the Hindu-Mahar riots illustrates this: the riots took place at the height of antagonism fostered by Congress propaganda against Ambedkar for remaining aloof from the national movement. Later years saw Ambedkar arguing that the Socialist Caste Federation (SCF) would transform itself into a backward caste federation if necessary, making his first post-independence political alliance with the socialists who were gaining an OBC base. When Congress offered him a position as head of the Drafting Committee of the Constitution, and later as Minister of Law, he accepted it only to resign. Ambedkar had founded three political parties during his lifetime, the Independent Labour Party, the SCF and finally the Republican Party of India, which he gave shape to, though it grew only after his death. Within the general framework of fighting Brahminism and capitalism, of attempting to destroy the caste system and relieve the oppression not only of Dalits but of all Indians, Ambedkar had thus used flexible political strategies.

This has to be emphasized today, when so many Dalits are either becoming emotionally tied to the BSP, arguing that we have no natural allies, or considering the Congress and BJP to be equally bad, or taking an even more radical-sounding position that OBCs are the enemy and that no alliance at all should be made! In fact, Ambedkar's argument that we must become a ruling community could not have meant that only the 17 percent of the population who are Dalits should rule over the others. Nor was Ambedkar's fight against the Congress, which was necessary, given that it was practically the only political force of the time he had to confront, one that meant he saw the Hindutva forces of his time as an equal enemy. This was hardly a question since the Hindu Mahasabha was relatively insignificant politically. The real fight was with the brahminical forces within the Congress, and this to him was symbolized by Gandhi. His differences with Nehru were less intense.

In recent years the political attentions of Dalits nationally have focused on the BSP. This has had some justification. Kanshi Ram's achievement in forming the party, his vision, was to try to build a party representing not only Dalits, but all Bahujans, backwards, minorities and Dalits—with Dalit leadership. This was an important step forward. But there was a simultaneous failure. In taking up the slogan, 'We Must Become a Ruling Community', the party began to act as if ruling were all that was necessary. We will form an organization of intellectuals, was Kanshi Ram's continual promise and aspiration, but caught in the traumas of U.P. politics, this never happened. Instead, it was a Congress leader, and a Thakur at that, who provided facilities for Dalit intellectuals to gather and formulate a programme, the Bhopal Conference in

January 2002, which resulted in the Bhopal Declaration and the Diversity agenda, now endorsed by international conferences of Dalits at Vancouver and London. This happened at a time when the BSP was falling into dependence on the BJP, and now, with Mayawati out of power and Kanshi Ram seriously ill, movement ahead for the BSP seems to have stopped. Kanshi Ram has carried the caravan of Dalit aspirations forward, but it is difficult to say what is its future even in its areas of strength, in northern India.

Now it might prove useful to look south. Tamil Nadu tends to be isolated from the rest of India by geography as much as by language. It is not that it has not been part of a broader Indian civilization; it always has been. Yet at the same time its separate identity whether we call that national or not has been very clear. The Tamil area remained outside of even the Ashokan empire (though it had absorbed Buddhism), and the ancient Greeks distinguished Damirica as a clearly separate region of the subcontinent. But Tamil Nadu's strong separateness has sometimes meant isolation, and this has to some extent been true in the Dalit movement also. It is time to rectify this north-south divide. Tamil Nadu shows us a political situation that contrasts both with the failing BSP and the stagnation in Maharashtra. The Tamil Dalit-based parties have not been able to win the kind of spectacular success that the BSP had, for some time, in U.P. But they face a very different situation. Where the BSP could rely on the numerical strength of its Chamar base—the Chamars form a larger percentage than almost any other Dalit jati and have faced a divided opposition—the Tamil parties have not only been split among two major regionally-based Dalit jatis, each fighting a reactionary OBC group, but have also had to face the tough Jayalalitha blitz. Their electoral success has been minimal and sporadic. Yet they have mobilized in significant numbers and have become a force to reckon with in the politics of the state. The Dalit upsurge in Tamil Nadu has been political and cultural, and is taking bold, experimental forms. Today, with the BSP failing and fragmenting and with the one-time centre of Dalit politics in Maharashtra in its usual doldrums, Tamil Nadu may offer some important lessons.

The articles in this book show the direction of these. Thirumaavalavan has chosen his alliance with the most Dravidian of the existing two parties in spite of the serious problems that exist as against the more brahminical forces. He has been open to working with the Left; it has been rather the Left, especially the CPI(M), that has rejected this position. His articles show the balance of his position and the occasional brilliance of his journalism. His observation on the issue of Sonia Gandhi's foreign birth, for instance, is devastating: if being born in India is what counts, then why shouldn't Musharraf become Prime Minister? He has written of the problems of an electoral system with only reserved seats, in which a Dalit who has almost no votes from the Dalit community but a majority of caste-Hindu votes can win (this is brilliantly criticized by another Dalit intellectual, Satinath Choudhary, who has been arguing for a system of proportional representation). Similarly, Thirumaavalavan has made a fierce attack on the anti-conversion law, noting that conversion went on not only to the so-called non-Hindu religions, a concept he mocks, but also from Saivism to Vaishnavism. From the time religions were formed, the right to convert existed, and that the Tamil Nadu Government is violating constitutional rights in seeking to prevent it. Is the governance in Tamil Nadu to safeguard religion? Or is it to safeguard humanity? Will this law that prohibits religious conversion convert the mind of him who forced another man to eat excrement? (p. 146)

Thirumaavalavan's stand on two major issues illustrates the importance of his work: The first is that of women's liberation. The connection of the Dravidian movement with women's empowerment has been much debated in the pages of journals such as the *Economic and Political Weekly*, with opposing positions taken by C. S. Laxmi, M. S. S. Pandian and V. Geetha. Thirumaavalavan does not refer to this debate; indeed, why should he? But his own position is clear. The favourite heroine of Tamil culture, Kannagi, on whom the famous epic *Silappadhikaram* centres, is far from a symbol of women's empowerment. Chastity is only a violence fabricated by men for the benefit of men and imposed on women. Tamil society's code of life has been ordered only central to that (p.60). It is an uncompromising critique of a major interpretation of Tamil culture from what is not simply a Dalit perspective but a feminist/humanist one.

The second important issue is to analyse and form political strategies to deal with the Dravidian (non-Brahmin) movement and the Tamil (Dravidian) identity: what have these meant, and what do these mean, for Dalits? In regard to the practical question of making alliances, Thirumaavalavan's position of allying with the DMK shows a clear choice in spite of the conflicts and contradictions that exist; he has chosen an alliance against the greater enemy, the brahminical and tyrannical AIADMK of Jayalalitha.[1] But what of the analytical issues? Why has Tamil Nadu, once so apparently progressive in its Tamil nationalism and anti-caste movements, become today the scene of such great violence against Dalits? It is not only a question for Dalits, of course, but for all those concerned about the fate of anti-caste movements in India: for Tamil Nadu, this means either that the Tamil non-Brahmin movement was never as progressive as we thought, or that for some other reason it fell seriously short of attaining its goals. The brutal conflict between OBCs (Yadavs, etc.) and Dalits in U.P. can be understood at least partially in view of the fact that historically these sections mobilized only under a Sanskritizing framework. But what has happened to OBCs in the land of the Self-Respect movement, and what has the strong force of Tamil culture meant historically?

On these issues there is an ongoing intense debate among Tamil Dalits themselves. There is a strong section of Tamil Dalit intellectuals who are highly critical of Periyar himself, arguing that the non-Brahmin/Self-Respect movement under his leadership never did more than seek to replace Brahmin by non-Brahmin dominance. This is backed up by various specific charges. Another group taking many arguments from the early twentieth-century Buddhist leader

Iyothee Thass claims that Tamil culture is itself as oppressive as Sanskrit culture. Such intellectuals look to a Sakyan identity for Dalits, an all-India heritage dating back to the time of Buddha and contrasting both with Sanskritic culture and Tamil culture.

Here Thirumaavalavan's position seems more balanced. Periyar was progressive, he argues, in his anti-Brahminism, his rationalism, his opposition to the caste system. Thirumaavalavan thus identifies the aspirations of Dalits with Dravidian/Tamil culture, seeing Dalits as the major force to carry forward a radical Tamil identity, rather than seeking to negate it. The major degeneration from the ideals of the earlier movement came, Thirumaavalavan argues, after independence with an initial compromise made by the DMK under Karunanidhi's leadership, a compromise that only paved the ground for the complete reversal under the self-proclaimed Brahmin woman Jayalalitha. With her, Dravidianism has turned into its opposite, with only the name AIADMK remaining as a hollow mockery.

It could be asked whether it is sufficient to look only to post-independence developments. In regard to Periyar himself, for example, I was struck during my last visit to Madurai and Chennai with the defensiveness of non-Brahmins on that issue, as if criticism were something that ought not to have been made. It was also surprising to find Periyar's writings little available in contrast to the Maharashtra Government's circulation of Phule's writings (at 150,000 sales of the few books from the Maharashtra Government committee that publishes and translates his writings, he stands behind only Ambedkar as a best-selling author in the state). If Periyar as a man and a leader had limitations, these have to be openly discussed. What strikes me as someone knowing Maharashtra well, is that there were significant differences between Phule and Periyar, for instance, in regard to Phule's own daring behaviour on the caste issue: throwing open his household well to neighbouring untouchables in the nineteenth century, adopting a child of a Brahmin widow (for which he was boycotted for a time by his own caste people) and so on. There were also important contrasts between Ambedkar and the contemporary Dalit leadership in pre-independence Tamil Nadu: Ambedkar's lieutenants at the time were without much mass base of their own, and the towering leader with a mass base, M.C. Rajah, continually sided with the Hindu Mahasabha and in general was Ambedkar's opponent at many points of time. All of this history has had consequences—which is not to say that history constitutes simply a burden which frames and sets limits to the present. It may indeed be that dialectically the democratic achievements made in Maharashtra in the time of Phule and Ambedkar have now reached the point of stagnation while the next step ahead for Dalit politics and the anti-caste movement generally lies mainly outside Maharashtra.

In regard to Dalits relations with Tamil culture, here Thirumaavalavan takes his stand decisively in identifying with that culture. He calls for changes of names from Aryan-Sanskritic to true Tamil forms; he describes Vaishnavism and Saivism as basically Tamil religions which have been captured by the brahminic forces; and he supports the cause of the LTTE, if not their methods. Again, looking at Dalits as the true leaders of a regional/national culture (and thus of the masses of people, primarily non-brahmins, who constitute it) rather than separating themselves from it is, I think, a correct one. However, there are nevertheless a few problems.

On the question of name changes, for instance, we might ask if Dalits and other strong Tamils (Tamilists?) are changing away from Sanskrit-Aryan forms only, or from Prakrit-Pali Bahujan forms as well? Are they adopting only an elite version of Tamil? As an outsider I can only ask such a question; others must answer it. However, I do have some feelings regarding the issue of script. Today in India, people speaking different languages seem to feel they also have to have a different script. This makes little sense to me, after all, the various languages of different countries in Europe share a script, and this in itself makes communication much easier. In India, all the scripts are descendants of what is called Brahmi, the script of the Ashokan inscriptions and later cave inscriptions throughout the country. They have varied over time. Why is it necessary to keep that variation fixed as if identity depended on some particular curves of letters? Maharashtrians, for instance, are kept alienated from Kannada-speakers and Telugu-speakers, their very near neighbours by the fact of a different script, whereas Nagari (Devanagari) allows easy communication northwards. Doesn't this unnecessarily isolate the south and other regions? Shouldn't we think about one script that could be used to write all the languages of India (including Urdu)?

There are some other contradictions in the Tamil nationalist position, not contradictions of Thirumaavalavan, but of anyone holding this position. For instance, it is said that the Indus civilization was Dravidian, but at the same time the Tamils of Tamil Nadu today seem to want to have an exclusive claim over it. Why? Dravidians were at one time spread over all of India; they are still, even if today they don't all speak a Dravidian language! When Ambedkar took the position that Mahars were Nagas, it was in the context of saying something like this, that the Naga-Dravidian culture was widespread throughout the country. In that respect, not only Mahars, not only Tamilians, but the majority of Maharashtrians (to take an example) are Dravidians. Maharashtrian Brahmins and those non-Brahmins who want to claim Rajput or Kshatriya descent may not agree, but that is their problem.

Today the most well-researched recent Marathi book on Shivaji by the historian R. C. Dhere begins from his *kul devata* (family god) at a temple called Shikar Shingnapur. This was a deity identified as the god of Gawlis and Dhangars, pastoral peoples identified with Khandoba, who is in turn identified with the Tamil Murugan by the German scholar Gunther Sondheimer. One name in Maharashtra, another in Tamil Nadu, but a god of people with both a pastoral and peasant tradition. On the basis of this and tracing Shivaji's own visiting of temples, Dhere argues that Shivaji's lineage had a southern origin, certainly not a northern Rajput one. Bhosles did not derive from Sisodias, but from Hoysalas! The thesis is a bit shocking to many Marathas, but should it be offensive also to Tamilians?

Finally in regard to Vaishnavism and Saivism: Thirumaavalavan is half-right in claiming these as Tamil. Certainly there are radical forms of both religions, that is, there are strongly radical bhaktas who have been called Vaishnavite or Saivite, the Varkaris in Maharashtra, the Siddhas in Tamil Nadu, for example. But at the same time it has to be admitted that within both Saivism and Vaishnavism there are orthodox, caste-defending, brahminic trends, and unless these are fought there can be no really liberatory culture for Dalits and other exploited sections of the population.

Finally, we should salute the militancy of the Tamil struggle and recognize the justice of Thirumaavalavan's slogan 'Hit Back'. Winning human rights in the face of an exploitative and enslaving system requires struggle and normally violence; the question is only one of degree. In Vasant Moon's autobiography, translated as *Growing Up Untouchable in India*, he writes of the Hindu-Mahar riots, mentioned earlier, which took place in Nagpur in the 1940s, which was a centre of the Ambedkarite movement. These were in fact fights between OBCs and Dalits. The Mahar community in the city had some base in the textile mills, it had a few small businessmen, and it had many wrestlers who were a centre of the fight during the riots. The reality is that in spite of the police ruthlessly taking the side of the Hindus, who were in fact OBCs, the Dalits came out ahead. Afterwards they celebrated it in song: *we killed their young men one by one* . . . Some time or another the battle for equality has to be fought. In the USA it took a civil war which left millions dead to achieve the end of slavery. Is it any wonder that Indian Dalits occasionally use intemperate language? In fact their struggle has been amazingly non-violent.

In both the USA and India, the fight for equality, against racism, casteism, patriarchy, economic exploitation continues; it is incomplete yet it has a history and the stages in this fight are important. Voices of this struggle are emerging even stronger today than ever before, and they are making their impact in economics and in politics as well as culturally. That is the importance of this translation of Thirumaavalavan's work!

Let me conclude with a reminder of the radical Siddha Saivite tradition with a song of Pambatti Cittar, translated by David Buck in *Dance, Snake! Dance!*

The Four Vedas, six kinds of Shastras,
The many tantras and puranas,
The agamas which speak of the arts,
And various kinds of other books,
Are of no use; just in vain.
So dance, snake, dance!

We'll set fire to divisions of caste,
We'll debate philosophical questions in the market place,
We'll have dealings with despised households,
We'll go around in different paths.

The debate is going on, the different paths are being forged, the snake is dancing!

GAIL OMVEDT
09 Nov 2003

Note

1. See p 18, note 1.

t.r.a.n.s.l.a.t.o.r's n.o.t.e
CHE GUEVARA OF THE CHERIS

'Pariah', the degraded, contemptible English word for outcast, was derived from the Tamil *paraiyar*, one of the untouchable outcastes in Tamil Nadu. Among all the intricate etymological and linguistic renderings of borrowed words, among all the words from the Orient that charmed their way into English, it is a shamefully stark thing that the Tamil language had to provide to the world a word for outcastness. It brutally reminds us that Tamil society had not only the glorious tradition and classic heritage that we are today proud of, but, sadly, it had ingrained the worst of the Aryan caste system. In a society that measured untouchability with distances, it was decreed that the untouchable outcastes had to announce their arrival, and give warning, so that no caste-Hindu would be defiled. And the most damned of the untouchable outcastes were the Pariahs, who polluted at a distance of sixty-four feet.

Centuries later, erstwhile untouchables continue to announce their arrival, and continue to give warnings to caste-Hindus. But these are no longer in the original context. There has been a brilliant reversal, a mind-blowing revolution. Today, posters and signboards in cheris in Tamil Nadu hail and herald the arrival of their Che Guevara. Cheri youth bravely retaliate, aware of the consequences yet embellished with the courage to face it all. To smash subjugation and oppression, once-passive lay people, that is, ordinary people, have become Liberation Panthers, Viduthalai Chiruthaigal.

But who or what shall chronicle this bold uprising?

If we leave it to the experts, the casteist atrocities shall be blacked out and our bloodstains shall be whitewashed. Then, who shall remember our martyrs, who will celebrate our victories?

For Thirumaavalavan, who leads the Dalit movement in the state, this foray into writing is a historic compulsion. The mainstream has monopolized intellectualism with the disastrous consequence that there continues to be a brahminical mania over education, over degrees, over the lineages of thought. So if writing is left to writers alone, we are guilty of allowing a neo-Brahminism. Thirumaavalavan's writings do not conform to the typical mainstream stereotype of Dalit writing, which are expected of being characterized by tear-jerking narratives of sorrow and all holds-barred narratives of social activity. His writings have their roots in his work, they are at once chronicles, ideology, manifesto, documentation, denouncements, and criticism. If his perspective is unparalleled, it is because he enjoys a position of eminence within the Dalit movement: as the General Secretary of the Viduthalai Chiruthaigal, as an elected Member of the Legislative Assembly and as editor of *Thaaimann*, a best-selling magazine on Dalit affairs.

Dalits, who were once blindly fanatic about voting for 'the sun' (DMK) or the 'two leaves' (ADMK) have erased those mute identities to rally behind the Viduthalai Chiruthaigal. It started as a people's movement and boycotted elections, and yet, the decision to enter politics was crucial to protect their organization from being banned. Their radical ideology was branded as 'violent' and 'extremist'; casteist political forces aimed at stamping on them the seal of 'terrorism'. When the Viduthalai Chiruthaigal contested in the Chidambaram and Permbalur parliamentary constituencies in 1999 as a part of the third front combine, the casteist ruling parties and the state forces unleashed unprecedented violence on Dalits. Yet, the Dalits braved it out to vote, to accept and recognize Dalit leadership. In Chidambaram, in spite of all the rampages (p.111-14) that charred the cheris, Thirumaavalavan, the Viduthalai Chiruthaigal candidate, polled more than two and a half lakh votes. Despite their electoral successes, they still maintain the stand that parliamentary democracy is not a field for lay people. The Viduthalai Chiruthaigal have proved that Dalits cannot be scared into silence. Now, it is for us to sit up and listen.

I did the translation of his work because for long I have grieved over what the absence of translations could do. The first example that comes to mind is that of Dewan Bahadur Rettamalai Srinivasan (1860-1945), a Tamil Dalit leader who was a contemporary and friend of Dr. Ambedkar. He represented the Depressed Classes at

Translator's Note

the Round Table Conference, and had earlier started in 1893, a weekly magazine *Paraiyan*. Despite the greatness of his stature, he is largely unknown outside Tamil Dalit-activist circles. His writings have not been translated nor are his contributions to the Dalits addressed with due emphasis. The second and more conventional example that I want to cite is the case of Periyar. If Periyar has become a victim of opportunist, self-effacing intellectuals, it stems out of the absence of translation of his work. He is trapped within the Tamil and so, even those who have not read a word of Periyar, criticize him based on Brahmin brainwashing.

While I was engaged with my long-term venture of translating Periyar's speeches into English, the first detour was when I was asked to translate the Tamil Nationalist leader Pazha Nedumaran's speech about the Tamil Eelam issue, a speech that spurred the government to unleash the POTA on him. The second detour, in the midst of the Periyar translation, has been this book. And of all the three, I found this the most challenging. With its native metaphors and the famed flourishes of rhetoric, I find this is the most vivid.

This work involved not only the translation from the Tamil original, but also included preparation of the notes that accompany most of the essays. As in all searches, I had to battle the absence of information. I also feel the need to say that efforts were deliberately not taken to adorn or tone down for the sake of 'audiences' or 'markets': this work is not a rock concert, nor am I a half-clad artiste hungry for well-timed applause. The translation to English is literal and as exact a rendering as could be possible.

What I have learnt through the course of this work is that translation is, among other things, a process of loss. In its cover story on Caste Struggle, the international news magazine *Newsweek* wrote that Thirumaavalavan's 'stirring two-hour rally speeches have made him something of a cult figure in the region' (3 July 2000). To listen to one of his fiery two-hour speeches it to undergo a conversion, a transformation. Writings are a little different. Though longer-lasting, their deliverance is late. Printed words don't carry decibel levels or the charisma of a personality. Yet they still convey the anger and agitation, the rebellion and revolt. As a deeply personal experience, to translate Thirumaavalavan was to rediscover Tamil. Brahminical dictionaries, and the 'authentic' works present convoluted meanings for words of rebellion. These elitist productions ignore the language of the people. But Thirumaavalavan, speaks the language of the people, his rhetoric is in their language of revolt. This makes him their hero, their leader. Or in their own words, the Che Guevara of the cheris.

What moved me during the translation of the work was the dissolution of the ego, the absolute absence of the self in the writings of Thirumaavalavan. For a leader who heads the largest Dalit party in Tamil Nadu and who is hailed by the Tamilians worldwide as an icon of Tamil identity, all through the thirty-four essays there was no mention of the imposing 'I,' or even the egoistic 'me' or 'myself'. In times such as these, where authorship is about authority and unabashed almost vulgar over-usage of I's, this is an overwhelming exception.

Gayatri C. Spivak writes that what is demanded of the translator and the reader is a surrender to the special call of the text. The call of this text is a call to liberation. It invites one to take stands on power and resistance, oppression and transgression, violence and victimization, agitation and retaliation. As a translator, I confess, I surrendered. As a reader of this book, you just cannot stop short of surrendering.

Finally, on the book's title: Thirumaavalavan chose to name this book *Talisman*, for he felt that like the traditional talisman which keeps off evil spirits, this is intended to keep off and uproot the Hindutva evil. I find layers of meanings: in contemporary connotations, talismans no longer have to be pendants of magic and myth. They have long since metamorphosed into agendas of action, into the capsules of courage; a symbolism that is at once a reminder of sacrifice, of cherished dreams, of the journey towards fulfilled goals. Take the example of the talismanic cyanide capsules that every LTTE cadre wears, as a mark of his/her self-determination. The Tigers are now, on their way to liberation. Let there be a Dalit liberation too, a Panthers' liberation. Let this book be a Talisman to us, a reminder and reaffirmation of the duty of our lifetime.

MEENA KANDASAMY
03 NOV 2003

d.e.b.a.t.e

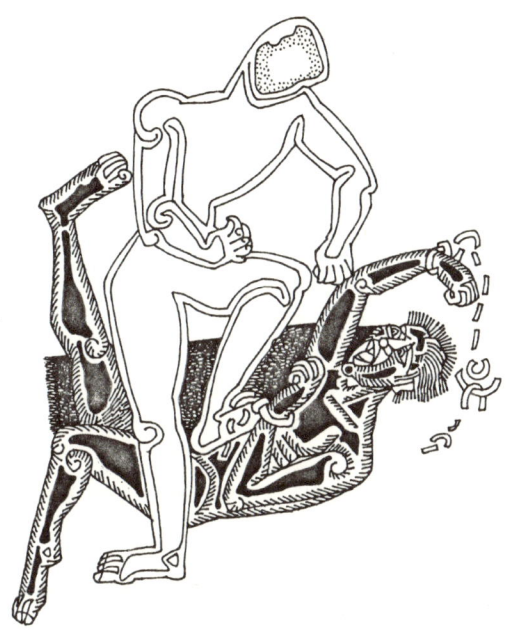

WHAT RULES THE NATION: LAW OR CASTEISM?

'Can a sparrow become a kite even if it soars higher and higher? A sparrow is a sparrow! A kite is a kite! Can the two become the same? It is like this only in humans too!

Are limits like 'upper' and 'lower' false? When there is inequality, everywhere and in everything, is it not there in humans too? Whether a man is superior or inferior, is it not decided at his birth itself?'

It is the doctrine of casteism to justify the differences in birth by blabbering in such a manner.

Are both upper-lower and superiority-inferiority the same? No!

Upper-lower is natural! It is inevitable!

Superiority-inferiority is fictitious! The attributed fiction of superiority-inferiority is casteism!

Casteism is only a fabrication—it is only an imposition. Even then, it did not remain as an exterior construction in the social structure. As a social structure by itself, the caste structure has expanded and permeated into the foundation of all fields like politics, society, and economy.

On one hand, casteism kindles the violent fury for dominance. On the other hand, it feeds slavery. Because of this, the fabrication of superiority-inferiority is continuously retained here. The onset of equality is to destroy such a superiority-inferiority imposed on human life and to bury casteism. In that war for equality, for ages and ages the endogamy prevailing in this society (in the Hindu society) has remained as the fortress that protects casteism. Intercaste marriage is a revolt against the system of marriage within the subcaste, i.e. endogamy. In the field of intercaste marriage, humanism imposes a death penalty on casteism. Casteism and humanism are directly opposed to each other.

Casteism—makes a human mad!

Humanism—makes a human mature!

The casteists are mad! They hang their own children. Recently in the state of Uttar Pradesh, a trembling newly-wed couple was hanged to death in the presence of the public.[1] Does law rule the nation? Or does casteism rule it? According to the laws, is it a crime to marry outside one's caste? Then, why were they punished? Casteism still rules the Indian nation!

In Tamil Nadu also, caste atrocities are rife. A few years ago, in a village called Echur, near Thiruporur, a young woman who married a Dalit man was set on the funeral pyre and burnt alive by her caste-maniac parents and siblings. The heart-rending cries of that girl drifted and subsided within the dark cremation ground. The Dalit youth, who went in search of his wife, was also burnt on the same pyre![2] What crime did these people, who were reduced to ashes, commit? Was this a punishment that the law gave them? Or were they given this punishment by casteism? Here, the reign of casteism itself takes place only in the shade of the law! The law solely attends to casteism! That is why, the law witnesses passively while casteism goes from village to village in lorries and burns down the *cheris* (Dalit settlements set apart from the caste-Hindu village)!³ The legal governmental agencies play a great role in preserving casteism. Even today, the governmental agencies like the judiciary, administration, police force, have not lifted even their little finger against casteism.

The Kandadevi chariot being pulled by caste-Hindus and policemen.

The judiciary protected casteism by releasing as 'Not Guilty,' a caste-fanatic landlord—who, in 1968, burnt alive forty-four people in the Venmani massacre—based on the conjecture, 'It is not possible for the landlord to do like that.'⁴ Even now, we are unable to pull the chariot in Kandadevi.⁵ In Azhagapuram, we are unable to enter the temple.⁶ In the Madurai district, even nomination papers could not be filed in five Panchayat constituencies reserved for the Dalits.⁷ Melavalavu Murugesan, who transgressed this in his constituency, was beheaded.⁸ In the rest of the four constituencies, the administration in kneeling before casteism, incapable of holding the elections even after five years! Powerless and unable to remove the coconuts shells, or separate tumblers in teashops,⁹ the administrative sector is hesitant, struggling and standing

These are not the ruins of any ancient civilization. This is a cheri in Thiruvallur set afire by casteist mobs

unconscious before casteism!

In Erampatti, near Alanganallur village in Madurai district, the people living in the cheri were chased out by the caste fanatics for having celebrated Dr. Ambedkar's birthday.[10] They are scattered apart and are unable to return to the village for the past four months and even today, the administrative department remains a passive witness!

Kodiyangulam,[11] Gundupatti,[12] Okalur,[13] Vandavasi,[14] ... in this manner, even today the police continue to force their way into several cheris to carry out rampages like the caste fanatics themselves. The police department itself occupies the forefront in protecting casteism and establishing it. Moreover, the police department also leads in unleashing state atrocities to control and curtail the people who raise and rebel against the casteist atrocities.

This way, innumerable people of the cheri suffer as refugees in their own land. They wander and run from village to village. But, the manipulative administration takes no notice of them.

Like this, on one side, state atrocity is imposed through governmental agencies! On the other side, casteist atrocity is committed by caste-fanatics! Is it not inevitable that people organize against such atrocities; they refuse to be repressed, and revolt? This natural uprising is only against atrocities and violence! Casteist forces continuously take efforts to politically sideline and oppress this, by branding it as violence, extremism, terrorism, etc. What is violence? Does it have any general definition? If the mother hen chases away the kite, is it violence? There are people here who shamelessly argue that only the hen chasing away the kite is violence! What is violence? The kite swooping down on the chicken? Or is violence, the mother hen chasing away the kite? Where is the need for debate in this!

In all directions one hears the slogans of human rights and humanism. But even in that, casteist atrocities are ostracized. They are leaping against racism. But against casteism?

What is the psychology?

When asleep, he slits the throats![15] For contesting an election,

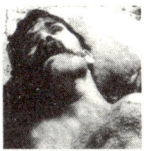

he beheads![16] For having married, he kills by hanging! For having entered the temple, he sets them afire! For having entered the pond, he burns the huts![17] He imposes the prohibitions: Don't give employment in the land! Don't give provisions in the shop! Don't provide water!

How is it possible to turn a blind eye to such atrocities alone? Even human rights activists are silent! How is that? Why is it that even those who scream in panic saying animals must not be slaughtered, are not even a little discomforted after seeing a woman, in advanced stages of pregnancy, being stripped naked and dragged in the streets?[18] What mental state is this?

Here, the dwelling place is two: *ur* (the village, the 'upper' caste settlement) and *cheri* (the Dalit settlement on the village outskirts). Why?... India itself exists as two Indias. In teashops,

(Top left) Murdered Dalit victims. (Above) The Viduthalai Chiruthaigal rally organized on 23 June 2000 at Chennai to condemn the Puliangudi murders and to demand a CBI probe in which over a lakh people participated.

there are two tumblers: tumblers and coconut shells. Even after death, the cremation ground is separate for the 'upper' castes and the 'untouchables'! Must not they surge up and question, 'Why is this?' That is not happening! What type of culture is this?

A few years ago, near Kumbakonam, a frenzied and murderous mob prevented Dalits from carrying a corpse through a government-constructed bridge on a public road. That bridge itself was destroyed and broken. In several villages like Kudithangi, for days the corpses remain reeking of stench and they are finally buried in graves dug at the back of the huts! It is customary even now!

In these days where human rights and civil rights are talked about limitlessly, it is impossible to imagine all this! Are all these human qualities? Why does anyone, including the political leaders not brag about this?... Here humanity has become insensitive to the level of saying, 'Casteism must never be debated.' If it becomes anti-national even to simply say that caste must be debated in the Durban conference,[19] the extent of casteism here can be understood! In that conference, racism can be debated! Must casteism not be debated? It is not shocking when those who justify casteism and caste structure holler like this. But why is it that those who brag of being democratic forces, have not opened their mouths about this? If not at the international level, must not casteism be debated at least at the national level? Only then, the answer to 'Does law rule India? Or does casteism rule India?' will be known!

22 AUGUST 2001

Notes

1. On 6 August 2001, a pair of mixed-caste lovers (Vishal (20), a 'high' caste Brahmin, and Sonu (18), of the Jat caste) were hanged in public by their family members in Alipur village, Muzaffarnagar district, in Uttar Pradesh because they had dared to fall in love.
2. Five years ago in the Echur village near Thiruporur in the Chengalpattu district in Tamil Nadu, a caste-Hindu Vanniyar woman, Indra (19), and her Dalit lover, Rajendran (23), had eloped and married. Later a pregnant Indra was called by her parents. When she went, her three elder brothers and parents, burnt her to death in the graveyard. Rajendran was also burnt

to death on the same pyre. However, in a gross misca[rriage of justice, all] accused have been set free.

3. The term *cheri*, in Tamil, denotes the Dalit settlem[ent which is] spatially apart from the *ur* which is the 'village' of t[he upper castes. The] demarcation of the cheri and the ur is rigid, mak[ing the cheris] vulnerable to planned attacks. The cheri outside the village is a continuing evidence of their outcastness. In most places in Tamil Nadu, the cheris are set in the northeast outskirts of the village; for, the wind blows from the southwest direction. The wind reaches the cheris at the last; this has been formulated so as to ensure that the wind is not 'polluted' when it reaches the 'higher' castes. In this book we often prefer to use the term cheri(s) to denote Dalit settlement(s), and cheri people to denote the Dalits.

4. In the gruesome incident at Venmani in Tanjore district, Tamil Nadu; forty-four Dalits—including sixteen men (ten of them under sixteen years) and twenty-eight women (twelve of them under sixteen years)—were burnt alive in a hut by the 'upper' caste landlord Gopalakrishna Naidu on 25 December 1968 for demanding higher wages. The Madras High Court set free all the accused and nobody was punished for this mass murder. See article 'Must Venmani Be Fenced?' pp.169-74.

5. In the three-hundred-year-old Swarnamoortheeswarar temple at Kandadevi in the Devakottai Taluk in the Sivaganga district in southern Tamil Nadu, Dalits have demanded, for over six years, their right to pull the chariot of the temple during the ten-day temple festival. Though the Dalits had always pulled the chariot alongside the Kallars (same as Thevars, an oppressor caste in southern Tamil Nadu) due to the Unchanai murders (five Dalits were killed due to a temple festival, see note 2, p.36) they stopped pulling the chariot in 1979. When they later sought to re-establish their rights they were beaten up. In 1998, the Dalits staked their claim to participate in the temple festival that was to be held on 7 July. The Madras High Court—following a writ petition filed by Dr. Krishnaswamy, leader of the Puthiya Tamizhagam—directed the state administration to 'ensure and take appropriate steps which are according to the situation, and in the interest of the administration to avoid an explosive situation on the spot and at the same time ensure that peace-loving citizens are able to participate in the rituals in a peaceful manner.' On the day of the festival, the police who allegedly feared an 'explosive situation' taking place because of the mobilization of too many people issued prohibitory orders under Section 144(2) of the Criminal Procedure Code. These orders were extended periodically.

Meanwhile, the Ambalams, the traditional caste leaders of the Kallars and hereditary heads of the people in four *Nadus* (ancient caste-Hindu judicial systems which impose punishments, issue decrees and economically control villages within its jurisdiction—for more refer note no.3, pp.31-32)—filed a petition before the Joint Commissioner, Hindu Religious and Charitable Endowments Board of Sivaganga, seeking their traditional right of pulling the temple chariot to be established. The Joint Commissioner sent an order on 8 April 1999 stating that the Ambalams had the right to pull the *vadam* (lit. rope) of the temple chariot after receiving the temple honours. This was challenged by Dr. Krishnaswamy and every subsequent year the chariot could not be pulled and 'maintenance of law and order' was cited as the reason. In 2001, the Ambalams refused to receive the honours at the temple, and the chariot-pulling was again not performed.

In 2002, the Anna Dravida Munnetra Kazhagam (ADMK) Government—which enjoys the bulk of the Thevar votebank—went ahead to somehow ensure that the chariot was pulled, because for four years the earlier Dravida Munnetra Kazhagam (DMK) Government had not been able to do so. On the day of the temple festival, amidst heavy police protection, Kallars pulled the chariot and deviously saw to it that Dalits didn't have any space of participation. In 2003, the Ambalams and their families stormed out of the temple after receiving the honours. Since their absence in the chariot-pulling would be a violation of guidelines, the District Collector declared that there would be no pulling of the Kandadevi temple chariot with a view of maintenance of law and order.

6. For several decades, Dalits were denied entry by the Vanniyars (the dominant backward castes of northern Tamil Nadu) in the Azhageswar temple at Azhagapuram village in the Ariyalur district. In this caste-ridden village, the 'two-tumbler' system is still active, and Dalits are not allowed to use the direct path leading to the graveyard. The Viduthalai Chiruthaigal had made arrangements and taken efforts for a temple-entry agitation. The CPI(M) was also in support of this. However, to ensure that the credit for this did not go to the Viduthalai Chiruthaigal, a local Vanniyar Sangam leader along with a handful of Dalits of the Pattali Makkal Katchi (PMK), a party of the dominant oppressor Vanniyar caste, opportunitistically joined in with the CPI(M) members and 'formally' staged the eyewash of entering the temple. This was largely possible because of the alliance between the CPI(M) and the PMK, a party of the Vanniyars. But the whole temple-'entry' episode stopped just there. After the symbolic entry was staged,

Dalits still don't venture to the temple for they are afraid of the wrath of Vanniyars.
7. The five reserved constituencies mentioned refer to the Panchayats of Pappapatti, Keeripatti, Nattarmangalam, Marudhangudi and Melavalavu in the Madurai district. For more about the election in the villages of Pappapatti, Keeripatti, see note no.1, pp.28-30.
8. On 30 June 1997, Melavalavu Panchayat President Murugesan was brutally beheaded along with six others while he was returning to his village after submitting a petition to the District Collector. Apart from the Panchayat President Murugesan, the Vice-President Mookan and four other Dalit members of the council, and another Dalit villager who came to the spot also fell prey to the attack. See note no.2, pp.30-31.
9. Despite the 'two-tumbler' system being a brazen violation of the Protection of Civil Rights Act and the SC/ST (Prevention of Atrocities) Act, it is an accepted practice that continues in teashops in rural Tamil Nadu. The shopkeepers owing to pressure from caste-Hindus serve tea to the higher castes in stainless steel cups and in cheap glass ones to the cheri people. In some areas, coconut shells, called *sirattai* in Tamil, serve as the teacup for the cheri people.
10. In the village of Erampatti in Alanganallur near Madurai, the cheri people planned to celebrate Dr. Ambedkar's birthday. So, they put up posters of the event and made preparations. The predominant 'upper' castes in the village, the Thevars, were incensed by it. So, around 11:00 a.m. on 14 April 2001, the Thevars entered the cheri and went on a rampage, they attacked the Dalits, set fire to homes, destroyed vessels and furniture, stole the TV sets, transistors and other valuables, and took away the cattle, goats, and hen reared by the Dalits. They abused the Dalits saying: 'How dare you men have moustaches? Why did you need posters and mike-sets?' A five-month-old baby, Ambedkar Raja, was seized from his mother and flung at a thorn bush. A newly-married Dalit man was savagely beaten up and he fell down on the ground. When he opened his eyes, they threw a stone on his head instantly blinding him. He later succumbed to the injuries on 18 April 2001. Fifteen Dalits who were grievously injured were admitted to the Madurai General Hospital, but no medical care was given. When the Dalits protested, they were beaten up and removed from the hospital. It was the third time such a clash took place in the Erampatti village.
11. A six hundred member police force attacked the all-Dalit Kodiyankulam village in the Tuticorin district on 31 August 1995. The village was relatively

well off, for, since the 1980s the Dalits there had gained from the money that family members employed in the Gulf countries sent back home. In the devious premeditated attack, code-named Operation Venus, property and consumer durables worth crores of rupees were destroyed. The food grain storages were demolished, passports and graduation certificate of the educated Dalits were burnt. The attacks were perpetrated with the view of economically crippling the Dalits and that is why all signs of wealth—fans, TV sets, blenders, tape-recorders, sewing machines, bicycles, tractors—earned by the Dalits were completely destroyed. The police poisoned the only village well. Behind this seemingly straight story is the interwoven nexus between the police officials, the oppressor 'higher' caste Thevars and the bootleggers belonging to these oppressor communities—who routinely give huge sums of money to the police as *mamool* (bribe). It has been widely reported that when Dalits of a number of villages met at Kodiyankulam on 29 August 1995 and decided, among other things, not to work for the illicit distillers, it came as a rude shock not only to the trade but also to the police; and consequently, the Dalits had to pay the price.

12. On 26 February 1998 police forces with the instigation and active support of the DMK, the then ruling party went on the rampage in the village of Gundupatti in Dindigul district, which is at a distance of twenty-six kilometres from the Kodaikanal hills. All the inhabitants of the village are Sri-Lankan Tamil refugees who have settled here following the Shastri-Srimavo pact. A vast majority of them are Dalits. For over the past fourteen years, they had been struggling for basic needs like a school, road, hospital, etc. Because their demands had not been met, they decided to boycott the twelfth Parliamentary General elections. This angered the ruling party which decided to wreak vengeance. On 26 February 1998, around one hundred policemen and thirty policewomen accompanied by four truckloads of DMK cadres raided the settlements, looted and destroyed property. Residents were assaulted; kerosene was poured into storage places and grocery items. Women were specifically targeted; they were kicked and beaten, their clothing was torn and they were molested and assaulted by the police. A pregnant woman who was kicked in her abdomen by the policemen miscarried her foetus. A child, who was hit on the head, succumbed to the injuries. Over twenty-five people were arrested, sixteen of them were women; and the victims were kept in police custody for a month's time.

13. On 1 December 1998, a police force numbering about three hundred attacked the cheri in the Ogalur village within the Mangalamedu police

station limits in the Perambalur district. Sixty-nine people, including thirty-four women and six children were imprisoned on the false charge that they threw petrol bombs on the police.

Background: The Viduthalai Chiruthaigal (Liberation Panthers) had planned a rally on 'Land Rights for Dalits' in the Cuddalore district on 28 September 1998. Following the Government's requests, the procession was shifted to October, but again permission was denied citing caste clashes. Next, a procession on 16 November 1998 was planned, this time permission was denied saying this was a caste procession, whereas people of an oppressor caste (Vanniyars) had taken a procession on 30 August 1998 with state permission. Because of the Government's anti-Dalit policy of denying permission to even hold a rally, the Viduthalai Chiruthaigal went ahead and announced that come what may, a procession would be taken out in the Cuddalore district on 6 December 1998, the death-anniversary of Dr. Ambedkar. The Tamil Nadu Government immediately convened an all-party meeting and decided that no caste rally would be permitted. So the decision of the Viduthalai Chiruthaigal to go ahead with its procession became a challenge to the Government. The police force was instigated to somehow stop it.

In the meantime, the then Propaganda Secretary of the Viduthalai Chiruthaigal, was jailed under the Goondas Act on 25 November 1998. As a spontaneous protest, Government buses were torched in Thittakudi, a town in the Cuddalore district that was adjacent to Ogalur. Therefore, the police began to unleash terror on the Dalits, and arrested Viduthalai Chiruthaigal members in the neighbouring Perambalur district. Already, Ogalur was a sensitive place and tension existed between the oppressor Vanniyar caste-Hindus and the Dalits over a disputed piece of temple land. A month earlier, there had been a clash because Ramraj, a Vanniyar man, had attempted to rape Chandra, a Dalit widow. Despite sustaining cut injuries, she managed to flee and reported this to the Dalits, who caught Ramraj and handed him to the police. Soon, Ramraj was out on bail. On 26 November, policemen in mufti accompanied by Ramraj, entered the Ogalur cheri at 4:30 a.m. and picked up four Dalit men on the pretext of seeking help for inquiry about illicit distillation in the village. The four of them were taken to the police station, and their names were linked with a bus-burning case that took place at Thittakudi.

Again, on 28 November, policemen in mufti visited the cheri at 11:00 p.m. and took into custody six Dalit men on charges of the bus-burning at Thittakudi. On 30 November, seven drunken policemen in mufti entered the cheri. On seeing the police, the Dalits who were watching television fled the place. Two 18-year-old Dalit women, who couldn't manage to run were groped and molested by the police. Hearing the screams of the women, the Dalits who had fled, came back. When the policemen threatened to throw bombs at the cheri, they were beaten up by Dalits in panic and subsequently the policemen left.

The next day at 6:00 a.m., a three-hundred member police team armed with lathis and rifles came in eighteen vehicles and descended on the Ogalur cheri. On their arrival, they fired three rounds of ammunition into the air. They hit out using lathis and rifle butts on the Dalits and looted their valuables, damaged property and inflicted heavy damage. They took into custody sixty-nine Dalits, including thirty-four women, six children below ten years and four men over seventy years. A woman schoolteacher who was returning after bathing was arrested. Also, a 70-year-old man, who was wearing nothing but his loincloth was arrested. This angered even the judge who ordered the police to at least provide him clothing. When a fact-finding team of a human rights organization went to inquire, the District Collector said that he had not known that any such incident had taken place. For two weeks no Governmental relief measures reached the people. Only the Viduthalai Chiruthaigal vigorously looked into the rehabilitation of the affected and soon held massive and large-scale protest meetings in several places in the state, condemning the atrocities unleashed on Dalits in Ogalur.

14. In a incident that involved murder and arson, plundering and police brutality, the Vandavasi Taluk in the Thiruvanammalai district turned into battleground for terrifying anti-Dalit atrocity. In this election related episode, members of the Pattali Makkal Katchi (PMK)—a party of the Vanniyars (a most backward caste concentrated in northern Tamil Nadu that often unleashes violence against the Dalits)—were not allowed by the Dalits, who feared casteist brutality, to enter three cheris: Kottai Colony, Mummuni and Periya Colony; so the Vanniyars couldn't campaign in these cheris. On the day the results of the election for the Legislative Assembly was announced, i.e. 13 May 2001, members of the PMK (the party's candidate had been elected in that constituency) descended on the Mummuni cheri and defaced and maligned a billboard of the Viduthalai Chiruthaigal by splashing cow-dung on the picture of Thirumaavalavan put up there. The Dalits of that cheri retaliated against the PMK.

Following this, on 16 May 2001 a token fast was conducted by the PMK under the leadership of Durai who is an MP belonging to that party.

The same night, the MP mobilized members of the PMK and caste-fanatic Vanniyars from the neighboring villages and attacked the Mummuni cheri and set fire to a few homes there. On 18 May 2001, a reconciliation meeting was held, in which the PMK MP demanded that members of the Viduthalai Chiruthaigal must be arrested.

At midnight on the same day, the PMK members in collusion with the police conducted attacks on the cheris at the Periya Colony and the Kottai Colony and wreaked heavy damage on property. An Ambedkar Centre in the nearby Mangalam village was set on fire. All through the offensive, the police and the caste-fanatics continued to speak derogatorily of the Dalits and insulted them by calling caste-names. As a direct fallout of the Vandavasi atrocity, on 24 May 2001 in the village of Punapakkam in the Tiruvallur district, a Dalit electrician Shankar (of the Vengal village where the PMK was not allowed during its election campaign), who was carrying out repairs on the electric poles was murdered as barbaric Vanniyar men switched on the transformer—due to which Shankar was killed instantaneously by electric shock.

15. In this gruesome murder that took place on 26 May 2000 in the M.Puliyangudi village within the Kumaratchi police station limits in the Cuddalore district, three Dalits were murdered for having raised their voice against the sale of illicit arrack. Gandhi (30), his brother, Vellaiyan (20) and Mathiazhagan (35) were murdered in cold blood in a gruesome manner; their throats had been slit while they were fast asleep under a banyan tree. The Puliyangudi murders was the result of violence perpetrated by communal elements and bootleggers who were angered when Dalit women in Puliyangudi launched a campaign against illicit distillation. From the period between 1998-2000, over eighteen Dalits, including seven women, had been killed in the Cuddalore district but all the cases had been hushed up. To protest against the rampant anti-Dalit violence in the district, the Viduthalai Chiruthaigal announced a total bandh in Cuddalore on 2 June 2000 against the 'anti-people' Government and to express solidarity with the affected. Thousands of Viduthalai Chiruthaigal members were arbitrarily arrested preceding the bandh under the guise of preventive detention. Cases under the Goondas Act was foisted on thousands of Dalit youth. The bandh was postponed following an all-party meeting in Cuddalore on 1 June, where all the parties pledged their support to the police in putting an end to bootlegging. In continuation with the protests, a massive rally to condemn the murders was organized on 23 June 2000 in Chennai by the Viduthalai Chiruthaigal demanding a CBI probe into the incidents.

Dalits who had come from the Cuddalore district to take part in the rally, were beaten by caste-fanatics on their way back. For instance, Mahboobjan, a driver of a van carrying Viduthalai Chiruthaigal members was attacked with knives. Many such instances of anti-Dalit violence shook the district, which was in a state of unrest for a week after the incident. Four thousand members of the Tamil Nadu Special Police Force and the Armed Forces were brought in to control the situation.

16. This refers to the Melavalavu massacre where the casteist gang beheaded the Dalit Panchayat President Murugesan, the Vice-President Mookan and five others. Even Dalit candidates who 'attempt' to file nominations in these reserved constituencies—where the oppressor caste diktat prohibits Dalits from contesting elections—face a grave threat to life. The Viduthalai Chiruthaigal candidates Subban and Poonkodiyan, who contested in the Pappapatti and Keeripatti constituencies respectively during the Panchayat by-elections held in May 2001, are unable to return to their homes even now, fearing threats to their lives because of the barbarism of the dominant Piramalai Kallar caste. See 4, 'Rule of Caste is the Rule of India,' on the state of Dalits in grassroot democracy, this volume.

17. Such instances are common in Tamil Nadu. For instance, in 1979 in Koothirambakkam village in the Kanchipuram district, the cheris were burnt because a Dalit woman had drawn water from the village pond.

18. The Marukalampatti cheri in the Dharmapuri district was razed to the ground and became a virtual graveyard because the Dalits dared to field their candidate P. Thangadurai in the Panchayat elections in the general constituency. On 16 October 2001, the day of the poll the caste-Hindus went on a rampage and vandalized nearly one hundred and twenty homes of the Dalits. In this incident the Dalits lost nearly one and a half crores in damages. A Dalit woman in her ninth month of pregnancy was stripped naked and dragged on the streets. She was kicked in the stomach and treated so violently that she aborted her full-term foetus. The nurse at the local Primary Health Centre refused to admit her and she succumbed as a consequence of the resultant complications and trauma. Those who protested against this were lathi-charged, and false cases were registered against them. The officers failed to entertain cases under the SC/ST (Prevention of Atrocities) Act. The Viduthalai Chiruthaigal undertook a massive protest and organized public meetings condemning this incident. See photograph, p. 35.

19. The Durban Conference refers to the World Conference Against Racism held at Durban in South Africa, 27 August 2001 to 7 September 2001. See 3, 'Will America Drop Global 'Supercop'ism,' this volume.

p.o.l.i.t.i.c.s

DALIT UPRISING
Will It Put an End to Dravidian politics?

That enmity has continued for thirty years!

Because of that reckless decision taken by the President of the Dravida Munnetra Kazhagam (DMK), Karunanidhi, in 1972, that enmity continues even now! Karunanidhi removed the immensely famous and popular film star M. G. Ramachandran (popularly, MGR) from the DMK.[1] There is no possibility that Karunanidhi took such a decision without knowing of its consequences. That decision must have been taken with the plan, 'Whatever happens we will face it.' That enmity is still continuing for these last thirty years.

Even though the DMK and Anna Dravida Munnetra Kazhagam (ADMK) have evolved into two very large political forces—to the extent that only these two large parties can alternately rule Tamil Nadu—many believe that the continuous and prolonged enmity between these parties is making both of them gradually lose their strength! It is possible to understand from the happenings of the last thirty years that a common principle for both the DMK and the ADMK is that 'one should defeat the other'.

Not only in politics, but in the world of arts too, Karunanidhi and MGR moved as very close friends. Their friendship was very intimate! In the late eighties, when MGR's health was affected and he was admitted to the Brooklyn Hospital in America, the announcement that Karunanidhi released was extremely heart-rending and everybody was touched by it! It was moving when Karunanidhi wrote about the friendship existing between himself and MGR: 'I greatly value and feel proud of my forty-year friendship with my affectionate friend MGR more than my twelve-year enmity with him.'

The damned politics alone kindled that enmity and created the friction and split in such a long-standing friendship and comradeship between MGR and Karunanidhi! Only the enmity formed in that manner, ripened to the level of MGR's and Karunanidhi's arrest and imprisonment! It didn't end with MGR's generation! It is being taken to the following generations also. Only as its continuation it has changed from MGR-Karunanidhi into Karunanidhi-Jayalalitha. Having perhaps realized that after MGR's demise only a person with an influential cinema background like him would have the power to oppose Karunanidhi, Jayalalitha was pushed to the forefront.

As a continuation of that enmity, after the demise of MGR, on 25 December 1987, Jayalalitha took up the leadership of one side. She was arrested and subsequently Karunanidhi was arrested, in this manner, the 'saga of revenge' is extending even today.

It is a renowned truth that MGR died due to ill health! But on hearing the news of MGR's death, Karunanidhi's statue erected in Anna Salai in Chennai was broken to smithereens with crowbars, by those whom he considered his own flesh and blood. Although there was no relation between MGR's death and Karunanidhi, they heaped and exhausted all their anger and sadness on Karunanidhi's statue. It can be realized that enmity and affection of individuals has permeated to that large extent among the cadres of the DMK and ADMK!

Even if both these Dravidian parties proclaim: 'Periyar's doctrine,' 'Anna's path;' Capturing power is their doctrine! Revenging is their path! They are adhering to this alone. In those days, there used to be a fierce competition between the DMK and the ADMK in forming a coalition with the Congress. Likewise, today there is strong competition on who is going to overtake whom and who is going to sideline whom in forming a coalition with the Bharatiya Janata Party (BJP) at the national level. No one can deny that the Tamil people and the Tamil land will be affected because of this attitude and enmity amongst the Dravidian parties. That is why, during MGR's lifetime, K. A. P. Vishwanatham initiated efforts to unify the DMK and the ADMK. That didn't take place. Now we can understand as to why that expectation and effort was meaningless.

For how many more years will the influence of these two parties among the Tamil people continue? Will not a strong alternative to the Dravidian parties be created in Tamil Nadu? If that is so, what has the capacity to take on that leadership? Will the Congress dynasty flourish once again? Will Tamil Nadu accept its leadership? Will the old customs and principles survive in the currently developing new democratic political situation? As an alternative to the Dravidian parties will there be an upsurge of new parties that branched out from the Dravidian parties itself ? Will the parties founded on casteism and communalism get this recognition? In this manner, several questions await answers!

It can be said that the Periyar movement with its basic doctrines like women's liberation, social justice, annihilation of caste, struggle against Brahmin domination, has in the last half-century left its mark of achievement in a notable manner only in the struggle against Brahmin domination. For example, in the political field, Karunanidhi's occupation of Rajagopalachari's chair was a great victory for the Periyar movement! Power sharing with the 'upper' castes in all areas like education, employment opportunities, etc. is a harvest of the Dravidian movement!

It is an undeniable truth that the consequent formation of a political upsurge among the backward and the most backward castes has further increased the oppression against the depressed people living in the cheris! This is a negative reaction caused because of the DMK and the ADMK not standing steadfast in the basic doctrines of Periyar! It can be said that these parties have changed to a direction against Periyarism, particularly because the oppressive forces that commit casteist atrocities against the Dalit people exert power over both these parties.

In this situation, the faith on the Dravidian parties has been removed and it has become an inevitable necessity for the Dalit people to independently raise and dare to assert themselves as a political force! Because of Periyar's impact, the democracy and power locked in the palaces of the elite, has reached the middle level castes. Keeping in the forefront that such democracy and power must extend till the huts of the subaltern people, the political upsurge of the Dalit people is expanding.

Will the Dravidian movements, particularly the DMK and the ADMK parties continuously support such a political upsurge of the Dalits? Will these parties realize that this upsurge will turn the dreams of leaders like Periyar and Ambedkar into an impressive reality? Or will the DMK and the ADMK merely make use of the Dalit organizations (as disposables) for the contradictions existing between them? Beyond all this, slogans with liberation potency are loudly heard in the cheris: *Democracy even to the last! Power even to the lay people!* O is this the alternative for changes?

02 SEPTEMBER 2001

Note

1. After MGR was expelled from the Dravida Munnetra Kazhagam (DMK) in 1972, where he held the position of Treasurer, he floated the Anna Dravida Munnetra Kazhagam (ADMK). He named his faction after C.N.Annadurai, the founder of the DMK and a former Chief Minister of Tamil Nadu. The ADMK was later renamed as the All India Anna Dravida Munnetra Kazhagam (AIADMK). Throughout this book, we use ADMK (as most sections of the Tamil media does) to denote the AIADMK.

r.a.c.i.s.m

WILL AMERICA DROP GLOBAL 'SUPERCOP'ISM?

In Durban, that spark of fire flew!
America came out of the conference platform in support of the Israeli Government. Right from the beginning of the conference itself the problem of the Palestinians became sensational. Even in the NGOs' Discussion Forum, which began on 27 August 2001 the Palestinians raised slogans, staged agitations, and turned on the heat in the conference. Video images, which described the encroachment by the Israeli Government and the highly devastating

attacks on the public, absorbed the attention of the conference. In the agitation of the Palestinians, more than the slogans against the Israeli Government, only the slogans against the American Government produced a great shock! Consequently, America quit the conference in support of Israel. Questions such as, 'Will the conference itself continue? Even if it continues, will there be any use in that?' arose because of this. After members of the conference committee held conciliatory talks with the representatives of the American Government, a few representatives alone came forward to participate on behalf of the American Government.

The Israelies accused that this conference itself was only a racist conference. To that extent, they too were brimming with bitterness and frustration. Zealous speeches delivered by famous international leaders like Fidel Castro, in support of Palestinians and against the governments of Israel and America shook the conference itself. In the valedictory speech delivered at the conclusion of the NGOs Conference, every single word of Fidel Castro made each and every Palestinian jump with joy. At the conference when countries aligned together in support of the Palestinians, it kindled the anger of the Israeli and American Governments. That is why both the countries walked out of the conference. Only then, that fire-spark flew. It is possible to speculate from America's hunt for Osama Bin Laden that there might be a connection between that spark of fire and the great fire continuing to burn in America.

The world stands open-mouthed at this attack on the 'International Bully'. America itself that has intimidated all the countries in the world! Moreover, it is a great shock when America points out that an individual committed this earth-shattering horror. While observing that this superpower is readying for war and has collected its entire prowess and strength against him, it is confusing if all this is real or imaginary? Is Osama Bin Laden strong to the level of making the all-powerful America shiver?

What is his background? Did this attack take place because the American Government helps the Israeli Government? Or is there any other reason? If that is so, why do the Palestinians exchange sweets and dance in joy? If this attack took place in support of the Palestinians why does Yasser Arafat condemn, instead of welcoming it? Why does the Taliban Government adamantly maintain, 'Even if Afghanistan itself is destroyed and razed to ashes, we will not betray Bin Laden?' Why have they publicly proclaimed that they are ready to wage a holy war against the American Government? Where will this end? Will a World War break out? It is being said that a bargain is taking place between Pakistan and America: For attacking Afghanistan by being positioned in Pakistan, America must necessarily retrieve Kashmir from India and give it to Pakistan. Is it true? People are panic-stricken in the midst of several questions like this.

Palestinians protest against Israel at the World Conference Against Racism (WCAR)

Under the assumption that 'all those who are bearded are Muslims', people are being hounded; this racism is rampant in every part of America. A bearded Sikh hailing from India became a victim of such racism. What a cruelty!

In order to put a full stop to such terrorism, one hundred and eighty-five countries met in Durban and held discussions for two weeks. How many million dollars were poured into this! For how many hours heated debates took place. All that became a wasteful expenditure! Just five days after the conference, not only Pentagon—the military headquarters of the American Government—and the World Trade Center, but also the intention of the World Conference Against Racism and the efforts of the UN crumbled and went up in smoke! Any vengeance or oppression or exploitation or supremacy must not be permitted to take place in the name of colour, in the name of race, in the name of gender, in the name of class, in the name of caste, in the name of culture, in any manner. It was to abolish such discrimination entirely that the Durban conference was organized.

Already in the years 1978, 1983 these conferences had taken place in Geneva. The third conference was the Durban conference. Only in this conference, majority of the nations have participated. Thirty-nine types of problems were discussed in this. All types of activities against human rights will spring forth as the terrorism called 'racism'; so, 'only through the protection of human rights, terrorism can be prevented'—this was the fundamental principle of the Durban conference.

But the UN assembly that conducted this conference has itself given the 'go-ahead' signal for a terrorism against another terrorism. The question arises if the UN can abet the terrorism of the superpower in order to annihilate the terrorism of the individual called Bin Laden? State terrorism alone is the basis for all terrorisms. Only the terrorism of the superpowers, which was internationally spread through colonialism, has turned against America and taken revenge on its innocent people. Unless a review of the external affairs policy of the first world countries like America takes place, a full stop cannot be put to such terrorism.

Without the first world countries dropping their hegemonic 'bully culture' of poking their nose in every corner, in every nook and cranny of the world and scratching with the gory claws of their military; how can the terrorism called racism be annihilated? The terrorism of the superpowers did not spare even tiny countries like Cuba and Vietnam! What is the use of conducting Durban conferences without finding ways to destroy State terrorism—Superpower terrorism? Instead of concentrating on retaliation in order to establish its international hooliganism, will the American Government review its external affairs policy? Will it show the way for world peace?

10 October 2001

g.r.a.s.s.r.o.o.t.s

RULE OF CASTE IS THE RULE OF INDIA!

Again, the same atrocity in Madurai district!
 In the Panchayat constituencies of Pappapatti, Keeripatti and Nattarmangalam reserved for the cheri people, even the nomination papers could not be filed by them.[1] The people could not even talk a word to the reporters and members of human rights organizations who had gone to inquire regarding this. To that extent, the threats of the oppressive casteist forces are rampant there. Last week, in a very frightened manner the people there told members

of a human rights organization who went to meet them, 'We want to contest the elections. But there is no security for our life.'

Because of this, a few hours after the members of the human rights organization left the place, the casteist forces entered the cheri, attacked barbarically, plundered the property and crushed and destroyed the huts. Even in this situation no measures were taken against those indulging in violence. It remains customary for the state agencies to become impaired only when atrocities are committed against the cheri people. The approach of the Government is the same in such conflicts irrespective of the party that is ruling.

During the last Panchayat elections, it was the rule of the DMK! Then, in the same five Panchayats: Pappapatti, Keeripatti, Nattarmangalam, Marudhangudi, Melavalavu, Dalits were prevented from filing nomination papers. In Melavalavu alone, with the support of the Viduthalai Chiruthaigal, the nomination papers were filed and Murugesan was elected.[2] Since he violated the village's orders—not to file nomination papers—he was massacred along with seven others. But again, Raja was elected as the President and in Melavalavu, the political rights of the Dalits was established.

Even after the completion of five years it was not possible to hold elections in the remaining four places. At that time the DMK Government did not show concern in controlling and curtailing the illegal, anti-democratic casteist forces that prevented Dalits from even filing nomination papers. That is why in Melavalavu, the problem ended in a brutal massacre. When Melavalavu was announced as a reserved constituency, casteist forces indulged in violence by picketing and attacking Government employees, and demanded that it be made into a general constituency.

They laid down the precondition that none of the Dalits should file nomination papers and if they violated, they would be killed. Besides, the cheri people were asked to come to the village pasture, made to swear that they would not contest the elections and one by one, they were made to prostrate and pray. Because a few youths

Viduthalai Kalam (Field of Liberation) in Melavalavu erected by Viduthalai Chiruthaigal in memory of Melavalavu President K. Murugesan(top right) and six others (from left) Vice-President K. Mookan, K. Raja, O. Sevugamoorthy, and M. Bhupathy, K. Chelladurai and A. Soundararajan who lost their lives to establish the political rights of Dalits.

filed their nomination papers in violation of this, the cheris were set on fire. The caste-Hindus refused to hire the Dalits as coolies. They prohibited Dalits from walking on the streets, from using the village outskirts for grazing animals and from buying provisions from the shops! All those who had filed their papers, including Murugesan, were threatened and forced to withdraw their nomination! No action was taken by the Government though

The Melavalavu memorial

complaints were lodged with the police and the revenue officials on all of this. After the next announcement of the election commission, once again nomination papers were filed and the election took place. If strict proceedings had been taken on such casteist forces in the beginning itself, would their atrocities have gone to the extent of murder? Would it have gone to the extent of beheading Melavalavu Murugesan and flinging his severed head into a well, amidst the furious clamor: *Thalai irundhaal thaane thalaivan* (lit. only if he has his head, he can be a Panchayat head)? Would it have been possible for them to cackle in the very peacemaking meeting conducted by the officials, 'A *Paraiyan* may occupy the chair of the President of India, but how can we allow a *Paraiyan* to sit on the chair of a Panchayat President that we have sat on?'

The apathetic approach of the officials during the DMK's rule, is continuing in the same manner in the ADMK rule also! It is an agonizing matter that both then and now, the Government officials are providing the explanation, 'No one threatened the cheri people in those villages. Only the cheri people do not want to file their nomination papers.' It is not understood why governmental agencies display hesitation in pointing not a gun, but a mere finger against the oppressive casteist forces?

The wonder of the post of President of the village Panchayat being auctioned and the highest bidder being elected takes place only in the southern districts of Tamil Nadu. This action is not bound by the general democratic conventions in practice. Although the Government passively witnesses this too, it is not coming forward to prevent it. In the erstwhile Madurai and Ramanathapuram districts even today the *Nadu Kattamaippu* (lit. a parallel extra-constitutional casteist 'state' administrative system for clusters of villages)[3] method is in practice, which is also one reason for such activities. Within the state of Tamil Nadu, several 'states' exist only in the southern districts.

The functioning of those 'states' is not under the control of the Tamil Nadu Government. Its rules, inquiries, verdicts, punishments — everything, function independent of the Tamil Nadu Government. They are determined to safeguard the casteist structures. On that basis only, in a place called Siruvatchi, near Devakottai, the administration of the Muthu Nadu—imposed and executed a death sentence on Subbu of Madakottai village for having organized and guided Dalit people in a temple-entry agitation.[4]

One feels like thinking that perhaps the Tamil Nadu state administration is not taking notice only because such a system of 'states within the state' which is called *ur aatchi* (lit. rule of the

Poonkodiyan (Keeripatti nominee)

Subban (Pappapatti nominee)

Election poster being placed on a haystack at Keeripatti. Caste-Hindus would not allow pasting posters on walls.

village (caste-Hindu settlements)) is against the cheri people.

It appears that such a 'state organization' plays a major role in preventing the absorption of new customs and democratic doctrines; and in safeguarding the old traditions and casteist hierarchical doctrines. Based on this, in Panchayat elections, cheri people are prevented from filing their nomination papers.

When democracy and power are prevented from reaching the subaltern masses, the Parliamentary democracy that is established in the higher planes is only a bogus democracy. The brutal murders at Melavalavu and other aforementioned facts only confirm that in the Panchayat administration, the cheri people do not have any role. Even if several representatives of the cheri people are elected to the Legislative Assemblies, Parliaments and Panchayats, they are treated as powerless dolls! They are unable to speak anything regarding the democratic rights of the cheri people. The State Government does not display any determination in preventing the atrocities against the cheri people. That is why, even without elections taking place, the *Panchayati Raj* has taken place in four Panchayats in the Madurai district. So, did they name this as 'village rule', because cheri and power do not have any connection? Then, we can say that not only at the village level, but the rule at the Tamil Nadu level, nay, even at the National level, is only a 'village-rule'.

24 October 2001

Notes

1. Since 1996 to 2002, the reserved Panchayat presidencies of Pappapatti in Chellampatti Union; Keeripatti and Nattarmangalam in the Usilampatti Union in the Madurai district and Kottakatchiyendal in the Narikudi Union in the Virudhunagar district have had ten announcements of elections but nine times out of ten no Dalit could even file his/her nomination papers. The dominant oppressor caste in all these Panchayats are the Piramalai Kallars, a subsect of the Thevars. They have created a morbid sense of fear among the Dalits, by issuing a decree that any Dalit who dares to file his/her nomination papers shall be killed.

    The Pappapatti Panchayat, with one thousand nine hundred and ninety-two votes, has a Dalit population of 40 percent. This village is the birth place of Mookiah Thevar, a leader of a Thevar party called Forward Block. It has become an issue of pride for Thevars, who question, 'How can a Dalit sit on the chair which Mookiah Thevar occupied?'—They are unable to digest this challenge to status quo. Further there is a temple here that belongs to the Piramalai Kallars and it has been a tradition that the first honors of the temple are bestowed on the Panchayat President. To these caste-ridden oppressors, it becomes a issue, for, if a Dalit becomes the Panchayat President they would have to honor him/her in a temple to which he/she has no entry.

    The Keeripatti village in the Usilampatti Union has three wards, and a total of 1393 votes. About 25 percent of the inhabitants are Dalits, and it was declared a reserved constituency because of the eighteen Panchayats in the Usilampatti Union, the highest number of Dalits reside here. Keeripatti is the processing and export centre for the ganja that is produced in the hilly regions of Varusa Nadu, Mayiladum Paarai and Kadamalai Gundu. Every year, several crores worth of ganja is processed and exported; this 'business' is the major employment for the 'upper' castes. No person of the cheri has any connection with this. The police are very aware of this produce of narcotic substances taking place. The ganja is harvested from these places and transported to Keeripatti, where the leaves are dried and from there exported to other places like Kerala, Mumbai and Orissa and also to foreign countries. The police who have a nexus with these drug dealers also have a share in this. It is this gang which deals in ganja that prohibits the Dalits from contesting the elections in this reserved constituency.

The third reserved constituency in Madurai district which has gone without a Dalit elected representative is Nattarmangalam in the Usilampatti Union. It has a total voter-list of 1930 people, of which about 500 are Dalit votes. The State Government and various authorities maintained their false propaganda that 'there was no threat from any force, and that only the Dalits didn't want to contest'.

The Viduthalai Chiruthaigal decided to smash those lies, and in order to do so, made their candidates contest the elections. They took up this issue with the President, the Prime Minister and the Leader of the Opposition. Consequently, Subban in Pappapatti and Poonkodiyan in Keeripatti filed their nomination papers on 27 March 2002, the last day allotted for the filing of nomination papers for the elections to be held on 8 April 2002. This caused the Kallars to break the prohibition they had imposed. To prevent the candidates put up by the Viduthalai Chiruthaigal from winning the elections, they put up two dummy candidates in each of these constituencies. They threatened Poonkodiyan's brother and did not even allow election posters of the Viduthalai Chiruthaigal to be put up in these villages. During the election campaign in Keeripatti Panchayat constituency, slippers were thrown on the candidates of the Viduthalai Chiruthaigal, Government and Police officials who accompanied them. The Dalits of these two villages fled the cheris wishing not to cast their votes in the election. Of course, the dummy candidates of the Thevars, went on to win the elections. Within a hour of swearing-in, both dummy candidates Thanikodi in Pappapatti and Karutha Kannan in Keeripatti resigned their posts. Now, Subban and Poonkodiyan face death-threats, they can't go back to their villages.

In Nattarmangalam even nominations couldn't be filed because the Kallars had terrorized the cheri people to the extent that they couldn't even leave the village. Even though a candidate of the Viduthalai Chiruthaigal wanted to file his nominations he stopped because of fear. The Kallars didn't put up dummy candidates here like they did in Pappapatti or Keeripatti.

In Kottakatchiyendal, a candidate of the Viduthalai Chiruthaigal was taken and kept in hiding at Madurai where it was planned to file the nomination papers. But Kallars who came to know of this incident, brought his family there and frightened him saying, 'Your entire family shall be set on fire' and he was taken away. Therefore nominations couldn't be filed in these places though there were interested candidates.

On 15 September 2003, the State Government constituted a high-level nine-member panel to visit Pappapatti, Keeripatti and Nattarmangalam villages in the Madurai district and Kottakatchiyendal in the Virudhunagar district in order to facilitate the Panchayat President polls that were scheduled for 9 October. As usual, due to threats from caste-Hindus none of the Dalits could venture to file nominations. In the constituency of Pappapatti, the Kallars had put up a dummy candidate Azhagar, who won the 'election'. He resigned soon after he was sworn in. The Viduthalai Chiruthaigal deemed the whole exercise a murder of democracy perpetrated by the casteist forces for which the Government also lent its support. Therefore, this year it announced its decision to boycott the by-elections and dubbed the Government's move as an 'eyewash'. The Viduthalai Chiruthaigal called for a bandh in the Madurai district on 3 November 2003 protesting against the murder of democracy in these reserved Panchayat constituencies.

2. Melavalavu village near Melur in the Madurai district has a prolonged history of Thevar attacks on Dalits. In 1996, reservations had been made to the Panchayats for the first time. When the state Election Commission announced its list of reserved constituencies in September that year, the Melavalavu Panchayat Presidencies was allotted for the Dalits.

The dominant oppressor caste of the area, the Thevars, resented this because this change in status quo, apart from being an insult to their inherited superiority would also signal Dalit power; for, the Presidencies of the Melavalavu Panchayat would put into Dalit hands the rights of all common village properties. For instance, the leasing of the twenty-five fish ponds in the villages would fetch up to ten lakh rupees and it was precisely this kind of power that the caste-Hindu forces didn't want the Dalits to possess. Dalits were warned of an economic embargo if they dared to contest. The elections scheduled for October 1996 had to be cancelled since the caste-Hindu fanatics terrorized the three Dalit nominees, including Murugesan, from withdrawing their nominations. In February 1997, the Election Commission again ordered polls. Large-scale booth-capturing took place, the Thevars vandalized the ballot-boxes and threw them into a well and the elections had to be suspended. A week later, elections were held under heavy police protection for the third time and Murugesan (35), a candidate of the Viduthalai Chiruthaigal, won the election. The dominant castes boycotted the polls. But Murugesan was not allowed to function by the Thevars. They physically prevented him from even occupying his room at the Panchayat office. Only once could he enter the office: that was when he was sworn in and was accompanied by a police escort. He received many threat letters and he took everything to the notice of the District Collector. Many times he pleaded about the threat to his life and requested protection.

On 30 June 1997, when he was returning in a Government bus after having submitted a Memorandum to the District Collector, he was hacked to death along with six other Dalits: Mookan (the Panchayat Vice-President), Bhupathi, Chelladurai, Sevugamoorthy, Raja and Soundarajan. As of February 1999, all the forty arrested for the murders were out on bail and none of them had been prosecuted. Ramar, the ringleader of the Thevar gang was arrested only 2001. Only the Viduthalai Chiruthaigal extended protection and support to the Dalits of Melavalavu and organized the handling of the murder cases. Of the forty-one Thevars who were charge-sheeted only seventeen persons have been awarded punishment. For information about the legal aspects of the case, see note no.1, p.79-80.

3. According to Edgar Thurston (*Castes and Tribes of Southern India*, vol. 3, 1909, p.72): 'Portions of the Madura and Tanjore districts are divided into areas known as *Nadus*, a name which, as observed by Mr. Nelson, is specially applicable to Kallan tracts.' (Kallan, or alternatively, Kallar, denotes a caste unit which is part of the Mukkulathor, meaning people of three castes, which is now a dominant agricultural caste in the southern districts of Tamil Nadu.) Maravar and Agamudaiyar are the other two castes in the Mukkulathor community.

The caste name 'Thevar' is also used by all three of these caste groups (and widely by the media). Before the Kallars migrated to the Madurai region which was under the Pandya kingdom, their original homeland was in the Chola empire in Tanjore.

On the whole there were thirty-seven 'nadus' in the two districts, of which fourteen were said to be in the Sivaganga region ('nadu', lit. State, was a group of villages under the Chola administrative system). Each nadu is headed by an Ambalam (president of an assembly) and they adjudicate disputes that arise among all the inhabitants in their jurisdiction. This extra-constitutional practice continues even today. Their punishments towards the Dalits are horrific and demeaning and every time, more severe in nature than that meted out for the same offense to an 'upper' caste person. All are not equal before the eyes of this law.

They control the *neer* (water), *nilam* (land), *nidhi* (money), *needhi* (law) and *nirvaagam* (administration). Their permission was required for all transfer of lands. Although post-Independent India has seen a weakening of the nadus, which are states within a state, they continue to retain excessive power and authoritarian control because of their economic status and political power. The power they claim has no legal basis at all but they still exercise their influence. In areas under their 'jurisdiction', they don't allow anybody to sell land to Dalits.

4. Subbu, a Dalit of Maadakottai village—which lies north of Siruvatchi in the Sivaganga district—joined the Communist Party of India (Marxist-Leninist) in the 1970s. He started a teashop in Madakottai, and it soon became a symbol of self-respect of Dalits and later a school for them. Siruvatchi was under the control of the Muthunadu. The eight kilometres long Muthunadu lake—leasing it for fishing, for the trees, etc. would annually fetch tens of lakhs of rupees—was under the control of the Ambalams. He demanded the right of the Dalits to that lake. He was removed because he had transgressed the nadu limits.

He became the Panchayat President of Siruvatchi in 1982, winning the position from the general constituency. His election caused a great shock to the nadu structure. In 1992, he led a temple-entry agitation of the Dalits and they successfully entered the Muthunayaki amman temple in the Siruvatchi village. So, when someone was killed in Devakottai; the nadu, to revenge Subbu, linked him with the murder. He was arrested for two months. When he was out on conditional bail, on 13 September 1994, at 4:30 p.m. near the Tirunelveli bridge police station, he was murdered by henchmen of the Ambalams.

v.i.o.l.e.n.c.e

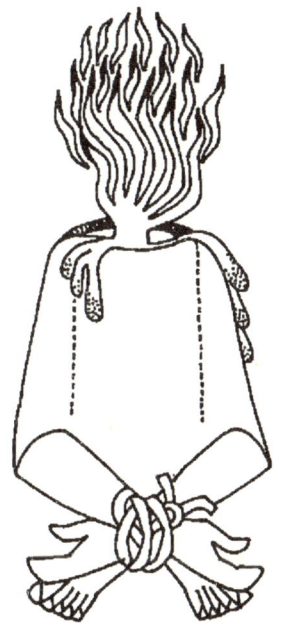

IS DEMOCRACY A DIYA* OR DAYLIGHT?

Is Tamil Nadu changing into Bihar only now? All these ages did it function like a peace-embracing monastery? Has not any incidence of violence taken place before this? From the massacres in Venmani to Melavalavu, what is the casteist rampage that is taking place here every day, every second called? Is the comparison that 'Tamil Nadu is turning into Bihar' fit only for the electoral violence? If it is so, will it not fit the barbarism of the last Panchayat elections, where Dalits were beheaded in the reserved constituency of Melavalavu? Is it also not an election-related violence? At that time, there was no whisper from any political party. Even now, the opposition parties have not uttered anything regarding the murder of democracy that has taken place in the reserved constituencies of Pappapatti and Keeripatti![1] What a wonder!

In the history of electoral politics, this is the first time such unprecedented extensive violence has run riot in Tamil Nadu! It is

Diya (in Hindi): small shallow earthern lamp

of course an urgent necessity to oppose and prevent such violence. It provides some comfort that a few opposition parties, including the DMK, are eagerly raising their voices of protest. Right from the day the ADMK started ruling, the fearless voice raised by the DMK to protect democracy and humanism is echoing in all fields. When a senior leader in Tamil Nadu and former Chief Minister Karunanidhi roars: 'The rape of democracy in the ADMK rule! Now, a people's revolution is the only solution! Soon, a revolution will explode!' it exposes the height of electoral violence.

If Bihar is a model for Tamil Nadu in such electoral violence, then the massacres in Venmani,[1] Unchanai,[2] Villupuram,[3] Kurinchankulam,[4] Melavalavu[5] and Puliangudi [6] confirm that Tamil Nadu is indeed the model for Bihar in casteist atrocities. It is a bitter truth that such casteist rampages and religious carnages are encouraged in anticipation of political benefit. Consequently, those who have served and matured by living not for themselves but for others are sidelined; the straightforward, pure, honest, democratic forces are marginalized, and the dominance and encroachment of the anti-people mob prevails over the field of electoral politics.

Terracotta horses at Unchanai Temple

It is not for anyone to deny that in the last Panchayat elections, extensive violence such as booth capturing, bogus voting, tearing of ballot papers, and attacks on the election officials was rampant. Unprecedented incidents of violence took place in six hundred places. Re-polling is also scheduled to take place in these places. And these are just the places where the ballot papers were torn. Apart from this, in several places, there were occurrences of violent incidents, but re-poll is not going to take place.

In several places Dalits were not allowed to cast their votes. In the general constituencies, where the cheri people have contested, they are becoming victims of planned attacks.

The Marukalampatti cheri in Dharmapuri district was enitrely destroyed and plundered and now resembles a graveyard. The people of the cheri have left the place as refugees.Likewise, because the people of the Veliyambaakam cheri in the Kanchipuram district contested in a general constituency, they were not allowed to vote, they were beaten and chased away, and they have also quit as refugees. In the general constituency of Sittampatti in the Cuddalore district a Dalit woman candidate who filed her nomination papers was threatened and forced to withdraw her nomination.[7] These have been listed here just for illustration. Several incidents like this have taken place. Such type of violence has not come to light.

A Viduthalai Chiruthaigal meeting to condemn the casteist atrocity that place on 16 Oct 2001 in the Marukalampatti cheri

During the last Parliamentary elections, in the reserved constituency of Chidambaram, one and a half lakh Dalit voters were prevented from casting their votes and twenty-one cheris were set on fire.[8] Thousands of cheri people were forced to leave their homes as refugees. That day, the tears and the blood of the cheri people flowed and mixed with the soil and their cries and screams rent the air. But, it did not come into the view of the political parties; nor did it reach their ears. What a wonder! Only as a result of everybody remaining with their eyes shut and mouths closed, five large anti-people gangs are encroaching and exerting their dominance over electoral politics. The five large anti-people gangs, that is, casteist fanatics, religious fanatics, the corrupt criminals, criminal gangs, and the opportunists, are orchestrating all types of rowdiness without any sensitivity. If the domination of these groups continue, the public will never come to cast their votes. If the poll percentage in the Chennai Metropolis is a mere 36 percent, it can be understood where the electoral democracy is heading. What will remain if we subtract the percentage of bogus votes from this? When 70 percent of the people have not voted, what type of democracy is the 'maximum among the remaining?'

In a way, it will be democratic if re-elections are held in places where less than fifty percent of votes have been cast. Is it the work of the Election Commission to mutely witness and conduct the election no matter what happens? Is it the work of the political parties to only seek benefit during the elections? Who will suppress and stop the anti-people gang that has infiltrated into electoral politics and exerts its dominance? Against the disruptive behaviour of the ruling party, can the ethical protests of the opposition parties put an end to this violence? If ethical protests are going to erupt in order to light the diyas of democracy in the cruel anarchic darkness of the ruling party through these agitations, will such diyas of democracy also be lit in the Panchayats like Pappapatti, Keeripatti and Nattarmangalam?

What is the use of the diyas of democracy here—when casteist hatred searches for light in the villages by pouring fuel and burning the cheris itself as expansive lamps?

More than being a diya, if democracy evolves into 'daylight', everyone will receive light. If democracy remains a diya, the power-crazy will put out democracy. Only when it radiates as daylight—as a great light source—can it provide the liberation of the masses and an end of the violent gangs.

07 NOVEMBER 2001

Notes

1. Refer note no. 4, p.7 about the ghastly lynching of forty-four Dalits in the Venmani in 1968. See 33, 'Must Venmani Be Fenced?,' pp. 169-74.
2. In May 1979, when Dalits in the Unchanai village in Ramanathapuram district came to know that the Thevars (the dominant 'higher' caste in the southern districts) were making arrangements for the celebration of the

temple festival, they demanded their right to participate in it. However, as they were denied that right they undertook efforts to establish it. In the temple at Unchanai, the festival centred around the practice of *kuthirai eduppu* i.e. taking freshly painted new terracotta horses, which were specially made for the occasion in a procession around the village. Both the Dalits and the Thevars had sought permission to celebrate the festival on 26 May 1979. The police who apprehended a possible caste-clash taking place, issued prohibitory orders under Section 144 of the Criminal Procedure Code. This problem was immediately taken to the attention of the authorities, who held talks with both the sides. The authorities cunningly decided that the Thevars could first conduct their festival, and the Dalits could conduct it later; this decision was very much in support of the Thevars. Thus, the Thevars were allocated the days 4-5 June for the festival and the Dalits were asked to take the procession on 20 June. The Thevars alone conducted the festival in a grand manner on the specified dates. Further, they went ahead and obtained a stay restraining the Dalits from celebrating the temple festival. The Dalit people, who were not a bit perplexed by these proceedings, appointed a lawyer to look into the matter, and were completely immersed in the festival arrangements.

On 28 June 1979, while a majority of the Dalits were away from the cheri making arrangements for the festival, a mob of Thevars numbering over 1500 entered the cheri, carrying spears, rods, sickles and knives and barbarically attacked the Dalits who had remained there. Thirty-two Dalits were grievously injured. Two Dalits lost their lives on the spot, three of them succumbed to the injuries in the hospital. The police force which came deliberately late arrested only 250 persons in this mob of 1500 Thevars. Although the police stated initially of examining 190 witnesses, it ended up examining only 88. Not only that, all the accused were later released.

3. Twelve Dalits were hacked to death in the Villupuram district in northern Tamil Nadu between 23-24 July 1978 because of the oppressive attacks of the dominant castes. The Vanniyars and Mudaliars went on a rampage which was sparked by a skirmish in the marketplace between Dalits and traders. In the consequent rioting, cheris were burnt and Dalits had to flee their homes. The court, as usual, set free all the accused.

4. On 14 March 1992 in the village of Kurinchankulam in the Tirunelveli district, four Dalit youth were murdered in a ghastly manner. The village, situated 22 kilometres near the Sankarankoil town, comes in the Thiruvenkatam police station limits. There existed a temple of the goddess

Gandhari Amman in eight cents of *poromboke* land adjoining the cheri. Since the statue of the goddess was plainly made of clay, the Dalits planned to install a stone idol for the goddess, so, they collected money and made preparations for the same. However, when the statue was brought to the village, the Naidus didn't even allow it to be off-loaded from the van because this was an issue of land, as well as an issue of status. Therefore, they blamed the goddess as being a *dushta devatai* (lit. vicious goddess) who would cause harm to the village. This developed into a severe imbroglio between the two communities. Though conciliatory talks were held by authorities, it was of no avail.

As a continuation of the escalating oppression against the Dalit people, a gang of the caste-fanatic Naidus murdered four Dalits The gang hid under the bridge of the Villakulam pond and hacked to death four Dalits who were on their way home. Their first victim was Subbiah (40), a woodcutter. Sometime later, six youths who were returning in two bicycles at 10:30 in the night after having watched a film at the town theatre fell prey to the Naidus' gang. Of those travelling in the first bicycle, Sakkaraipandi (28) and Ambikapathi (20) were killed, their throats were slit; while Anthony Raja, managed to flee despite sustaining injuries. Of the three Dalits coming in the second bicycle, Anbu (19)—who belonged to a nearby village and had visited Kurinchankulam to see his grandparents—was hacked to death while his two friends managed to escape. The Dalits of Kurinchankulam fled the village seeking refuge in cheris in nearby villages, fearing further onslaught by the casteist forces. The same night the police took custody of the corpses and the following morning, they buried the four corpses hastily in two graves.

The State Government—which could provide a compensation of one lakh rupees for a man who died in a stampede in a temple festival at Kumbakonam the same year (1992)—announced a paltry sum of ten thousand rupees as a compensation to the family of each victim.

5. For details about the Melavalavu massacre, refer note no. 2, pp. 30-31.
6. Refer note no.15, pp.13-14 about the murder of three Dalits in Puliangudi.
7. For information about the Marukalampatti cheri, see note no.18, p.14.
8. Refer note no.1, pp.112-14, p. for details about the ghastly violence that the cheris of the Chidambaram reserved constituency witnessed during the general elections for the twelfth Lok Sabha held in September 1999.

r.e.p.r.e.s.s.i.o.n

FIRST WE WILL PREVENT THE TERRORISM OF LAW!

'Why is the Indian Government in such a hurry? What is the necessity for a new terrorist act called the Prevention of Terrorism Ordinance (POTO) to be introduced hurriedly, overtaking even America? Will the coming of the POTO law scorch the entire terrorism? What happened to the Terrorist and Disruptive Activities (Prevention) Act (TADA), the Maintenance of Internal Security Act (MISA), etc., promulgated prior to this? Where did the Tamil Nadu Prevention of Terrorist Activities Act (TN-POTA), which was proposed by the Tamil Nadu Government in its previous tenure, go? Beyond all this, is the terror called POTO needed again? Are these laws for avenging political enmity?'… In this manner, there are widespread grumbles all over the nation! And the agitations of those concerned about the protection of human rights!

It is public opinion that those who govern use all the existing laws in the nation against human rights and democracy. In this situation, for a long time people have not allowed the introduction of new laws in the name of terrorism. People taught a lesson to Indira Gandhi who introduced MISA by gifting her a crushing defeat. Later, she even apologized to the people for having implemented that law. It is history that the MISA was only used to revenge the political enemies of those in power; nothing else was achieved! TADA, which was introduced subsequently, was also like that! TADA and MISA crumbled because of the protests of the public! The POTA Act, which was introduced in Tamil Nadu during the DMK regime, was quelled without even being presented! In this context, perhaps with the thought that political power was no longer necessary, the BJP Government has introduced the POTO as an emergency act. People compared the MISA and TADA acts that were promulgated after Indian independence, to the Rowlatt Acts unleashed by the British and crushed these laws. It is not understandable why the BJP Government—which knew all this history—brought the POTO.

It is shocking that parties like the Pattali Makkal Katchi (PMK), Marumalarchi Dravida Munnetra Kazhagam (MDMK) have welcomed this anti-people law of the BJP Government with their eyes shut only because they are in the coalition. As far as the DMK is concerned, it has neither absolutely welcomed it, nor opposed it. It has expressed its opinion that the law could be implemented after debating in the Lok Sabha. Consequently, it is known that the ADMK is making its moves towards the BJP under the assumption of a split in the DMK-BJP relationship. It appears that there might be a shift in the alignments in the sky of coalition politics, for, while the DMK is not wholeheartedly welcoming the law, the ADMK welcomes and supports it. It is being rumored, that the sensational rumor: 'Former Chief Minister Jayalalitha faces death-threat,' was spread in order to divert the people's attention from this. Showing this death threat as a reason, the ADMK has also welcomed the POTA.

R Nallakannu, TN President CPI, and Thirumaavalavan address the press after formation of the 'POTA Opposition Front' on 05 Aug 2002

This death-threat cannot be brushed aside carelessly. It is essential to inquire thoroughly! But is it proper to show this itself as a reason and welcome the POTO? The POTO law is crueler than TADA! According to this law, if anyone knows about a person suspected of being a terrorist, she/he must come forward by herself/himself and report it to the police department. Whether the police ask or not, anyone who comes to know about a terrorist, must go and give information, if he/she fails to do so, the law will consider that person as having involved in terrorist activities. Based on this, rigorous imprisonment for one year and fine will be imposed. Even reporters are not exempt from this.

Such a cruel anti-democratic section article is not there in the TADA. Next, the law allows for the confiscation of all the property of an alleged terrorist. Even if it is confirmed that he/she is not guilty it is not bounden in law that the confiscated property be returned to him/her. This is also a severity which is not there in the TADA. Moreover, this law allows human rights violations like reading the letters addressed to, and taping the tele-conversations of, a person suspected of being a terrorist. It is a hard reality that such transgressions will be more useful in quenching the revenging frenzy than in preventing terrorist activities. It has been promulgated packed with cruelties and terrors to the extent that they were not in the TADA. If the TADA is more severe than the Rowlatt Acts of the British, then the POTO is more severe than the TADA itself.

So in the name of prevention of terrorism, is it not a great danger to sanction another legal terrorism? Is it not anti-people to implement this law before getting the approval of the Lok Sabha and the Rajya Sabha? It is an immense cruelty that though the TADA law is no longer in force, those who were already arrested under it are still withering in jails. In the same manner, if the POTA is implemented now itself and consequently innocent people are arrested and later if that law is not passed in the Lok Sabha, what will be the condition of those who were arrested? Is it not very dangerous that the political parties approach this on the basis of political benefit instead of aligning together against this law, which is a tool of such state terrorism?...

Next, if terrorism can be suppressed by using the law, during the regime of Hamurabbi itself—who decreed the punishment 'An eye for an eye,' 'A tooth for a tooth'—would not terrorism have been prevented? Crimes and terrorist activities would not have continued during all these ages, right? But even though regimes of rigid laws have taken place, it is history that terrorism has raised its head again and again! Bhindranwales and Bin Ladens serve as symbols and evidences of such transgressions. Even though state terrorism annihilates Bhindranwales and Bin Ladens, it remains inevitable that the retaliatory terrorism alone escapes. So to prevent terrorism, the terror laws alone will not be useful!

Law—will bend itself for the powerful. It will kick the poor! What else can the law do? The law to a great extent affects the weak, innocent people who lack support in power centres! So before preventing the terrorist activities, should not the legal terrorism be prevented? At first, we will prevent the POTO! We will also prevent the terrorist activities!

28 November 2001

s.a.f.f.r.o.n.i.z.a.t.i.o.n

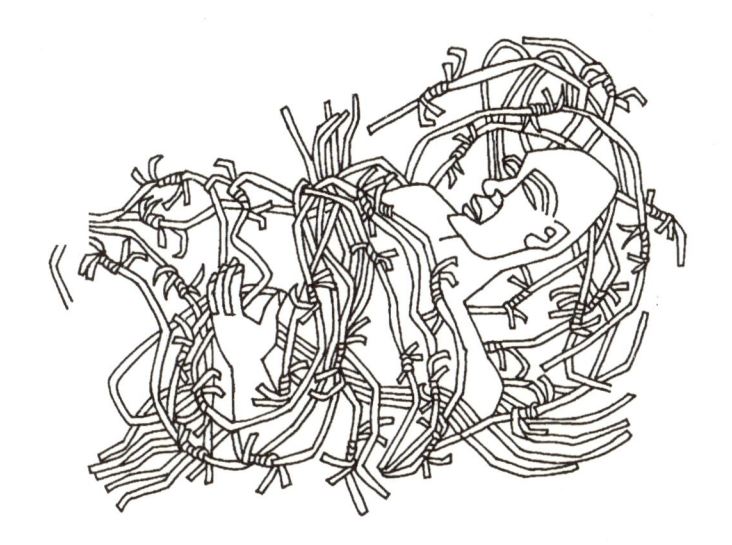

CASTRATION OF HISTORY

History can be corrected and written! But can it be concocted and written? Is it not a treachery done to the future generations to fabricate historical truths? How can hiding or manufacturing truths become history? Concocted stories replete with imagination and fictions can only be called *puranas* and epics; can they be called history? History is the chronological compilation of whatever took place, whether good or not. Instead of exactly chronicling the history of a language, or a race, or a nation, or an individual; is it not an unforgivable fraud to fabricate it then and there as per the wishes of those in power? It is a vast history that the ruling class is committing such fraud since time immemorial! It is a separate history!

Such fraud in history is being imposed on the education system by the BJP Government at the Centre. Even if does not come as a shock, is it not dangerous? Is it not against the future generations?

Even prior to capturing power at the Centre, the BJP that ruled a few northern states meddled with the education policy of the State Governments! It saffronized! It concocted history by saying, 'Aryans were not immigrants, they were native inhabitants!' And the truth was barred! Till now, the acknowledged history is: the Aryans are only immigrants who came here along with their livestock from areas of Central Asia through the Khyber and Bolan Passes, thousands of years ago! But the ruling BJP Government in Uttar Pradesh is brainwashing students and is saffronizing the syllabus by presenting the completely fabricated history that the Aryans did not come from anywhere and that they are only sons of the soil. On the same basis, the BJP Government is daring to distort the history even in the educational policy of the Central Government.

Here a lot of criticism prevails based on the allegation that 'Several of the histories already written by historians, are different from truth! Contrary to the truth! Fabricated! One-sided!' The history and life of the labouring people, the people of this land, has been entirely destroyed! And buried!

Not just stopping with heaping humiliation on the thawed, charred and oppressed people who are worn out by labour; injustices are committed to justify their debasement by blaming it as a consequence of the karma of the deeds of their past birth. All through the path of history are strewn such thorns of the fabrication frauds of the exploiters. In the exasperating circumstance where it requires impossible efforts to clear and clean all this, is it proper that they are trying to grow not just the thorns, but thorn-trees of fabrication frauds?

When compared to historical *contradictions*, the historical *concoctions* are more dangerous! They are capable of instigating racist, communalist and casteist hatred! So while historical contradictions may be allowed, historical concoctions must never be allowed!

The students of a class are taught the history of the Indian freedom struggle in one manner by the history teacher and in another manner by the Tamil teacher. The Tamil teacher teaches a lesson in praise of Gandhi's *ahimsa* struggle, saying *Katthi indri, rattham indri, yuttham onru varukudhu* (lit. 'without sword, without blood, a war is coming'). It is taught in the Tamil classes that Indian independence was achieved through an ahimsa (nonviolent) revolution—without violence and bloodshed. For the same students, the history teacher teaches the history of the Indian independence struggle in another angle. In the history classes, students are taught a history written with so much of bloodshed: about the struggle in Chowri Chowra as per Gandhi's instructions where an attack on a police station and subsequent bloodbath took place; about the lathi-charge during the Dandi march; Lala Lajpat Rai losing his life in a police lathi charge while opposing the Simon Commission; Bhagat Singh, Rajguru, Sukhdev and others being sentenced to death by hanging; Jallianwallah Bagh massacre; and Netaji's Indian National Army.

Teaching a student in the Tamil class that the Indian freedom was obtained without bloodshed, and teaching the exact opposite in the history class; these historical contradictions are not dangerous. Is it not a dangerous fabrication to say that the 'Aryans are not immigrants; they are native inhabitants' after completely destroying even the one-sided history about the 'Islamic *invasion* and Aryan *migration*?' This is not even a fleecing of the indigenous people; it is a castration, right? A man can be fleeced, but can he be castrated?

Is not such fabrication a fundamental conspiracy of establishing the dominance of one ethnic group over another? How can democratic forces allow this? They concocted that Gautama Buddha who rigorously opposed the varnashrama dharma-Sanatana dharma-superstitions was an avatar of Mahavishnu.[1]

Those belonging to the same lineage, are spreading the story that revolutionary Dr. Ambedkar who converted to Buddhism was a 'staunch Hindu supporter.' They are fabricating and informing that Dr. Ambedkar—who fiercely opposed Hinduism till his last breath—was a 'Hindu leader.'

They are giving discourses that 'Dr.Ambedkar, who wished to 'change his religion,' didn't go to Islam or jump to Christianity, but he only sought refuge in Buddhism, which is considered a branch of Hinduism'. Those who came this way printed and distributed pamphlets labelling Periyar as the sixty-fourth Naayanmar.[2] In this manner, those with the lineage of concocting history whenever the opportunity arose are engaged in an attempt to fabricate history even in the educational policy of the Central Government.

The explanation they are giving is, 'if history exists which says, 'Guru Tej Bahadur is a murderer!' 'Jats are swindlers,' would it not hurt the sentiments of the concerned? Only therefore we are changing all that and revising.' Can they change and rewrite history because it will wound their sentiments? Though the theory of evolution that 'man came from monkeys' is truth, it is disgusting. For that, is it possible to fabricate as human history, the *puranic* myths of the Manu Dharma that man was born from Brahma's forehead, shoulder, thighs and feet!

It is essential to correct history!

To concoct it is a treachery!

12 DECEMBER 2001

Notes

1. One of the most outrageous incidents of such co-option was when former Chief Minister of Maharashtra and the current Lok Sabha Speaker, Manohar Joshi, wrote in the introduction to the sixteenth volume of Babasaheb Ambedkar's *Writings and Speeches* that Gautama Buddha was the tenth incarnation of Vishnu.
2. Naayanmars is the collective noun given to the sixty-three Saiva saints who devoted their entire lives in the service of Lord Siva. Periyar E. V. Ramasamy, the Dravidian social reformer, was a staunch atheist. (For more on his atheism see p. 152). The Atheist Society of India, while condoling Periyar's death, called him, 'The Greatest Militant Atheist.' Apart from placing garlands of slippers on Rama and burning images of the Hindu gods, he ridiculed the Hindu myths saying: 'There are thirty-three crores of gods for twenty-two crores of Hindus which works out to one and a half gods for each person.' Such a Periyar was labelled by Hindu fundamentalists as being the sixty-fourth Naayanmar.

s.t.a.t.e t.e.r.r.o.r.i.s.m

POLICE TERRORISM

'The police are only a legally approved and uniformed rowdy gang,' — this is not what an unknown layman existing on some roadside said! Justice Mullah of the Allahabad High Court said this several years ago! How apt it is even today!

Suddenly, in the middle of the night the police entered the Chennai Law College Students' Hostel, and attacked students with cudgels and rifle butts in murderous hatred and quenched their bloodthirsty frenzy by going on a rampage.[1] The khaki-clad gang has again proved: *Ithu thaanda police* (lit. This is the police)! The doors of each and every room in the hostel were broken, those studying for the examinations and those sleeping wearily were blindly and barbarically beaten and pounded; and the entire students' hostel screamed its deathly shrieks!

Whatever did the students do?... A student who had eaten in a hotel that was opposite the hostel had not paid the bill, he had quarrelled and attacked a worker! Again, taking some more students to the same hotel he had caused destruction! If this is the truth, the guilty could have been identified and arrested! For this, should the entire hostel be converted into a bloody wilderness? Should an invasion have been carried out by those wearing their khaki uniforms and carrying cudgels?

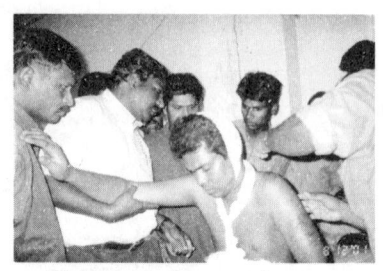

Thirumaavalavan with injured Chennai Law College students

To please the ruling party and to retain power, did they get only the innocent students?... What an atrocity! Is there no end to the brutality and ferocity of the police? Is there no limit to the police violations continuing here for years? What a cruelty!

When the voice of human rights is heard loudly on an international level, even now, murders take place in police stations![2] Sexual atrocities take place! The rulers, who must be preventive, are continuing their attitude of encouraging such conduct. Then, instead of considering human rights cheaply, would the police be afraid of it?... Not only in the period of the British, but even now, even today the police continue to be the henchmen of the ruling faction!...

Those who are in power are keen in encouraging and instigating the police to leap on their political rivals! That is why the powers to be are approving all the violations and rowdiness by the police! In the same manner, even the Home Secretary is justifying the murderous rampage on the students. How very dangerous this course is! Is it for the police department to be at the command of whatever party that comes into power? Only the interference of such party politics stimulates the violent nature of the police.

Thalli Kalpana Sumathi,[3] Chidambaram Padmini,[4] Athiyur Vijaya,[5] Orthanadu Rangamma,[6] Madurai Indira Gandhi,[7]... in this list today Tiruvottriyur Rita.[8] Like this how many women were torn apart by the police! Even greater than the cruelty committed by the police on Chidambaram Padmini who was stripped naked and tortured in front of her husband, was the evidence which the ruling party put forth that day: 'She is a woman of bad character!' Then, why will the police rampage not continue?

In Kodiyangulam,[9] when poison was mixed into the source of drinking water, the then ruling party said that it was not a crime!

The report of the Gomathinayagam Commission said that no mistake took place!¹⁰ Then, what is surprising in the continuation of these horrors in Gundupatti?¹¹

When seventeen persons including the infant Vignesh, were beaten and murdered, and the Thamarabharani turned into a bloody river, the ruling party justified the murders!¹² The Mohan

(Above) Police chase and charge at the rallyists who are swimming to safety. Seen in the background is the Thamarabharani River 23 July 1999. (Inset) The body of an injured rallyist is being lifted out of the river. (Below) Lathi-weilding police runing riot at the rally, most of the rallyists are seen in the river.

Commission report dropped a bombshell by alleging that only those who came to that rally were guilty!¹³ Then, why would police violence not take place in the DMK procession?¹⁴ If an end had been put to the murderous rampage of the Coimbatore police¹⁵—who poured petrol and burnt those who were gashed and grievously hurt and hospitalized on the verge of death—would the cruelty of shooting down the unarmed in the Chennai Central Prison have taken place?¹⁶...

Whom has the police not touched? Students, journalists...

Sankaralingapuram
Aftermath of the police rampage

women ... the downtrodden oppressed Dalits ... this way, people from all sides are leapt on! Can the atrocities committed on the tribals in the name of searching for Veerappan, be structured in words?[17] The unaffected, securely living people can argue adamantly that in the work of maintenance and protection of law and order, few transgressions are bound to take place! What is the need for a baton in the hands of the police who are meant to protect law and order? What is the need for crowbars? Recently, in Sankaralingapuram, the rioting police have ransacked and broken bureaus with crowbars![18]

The approach of the political parties and the democratic organizations towards such atrocities is on an opportunistic basis... When they are the opposition parties they oppose and when they are the ruling party they appreciate! This approach of the political parties approves of the violations of state instruments like the police.

When an atrocity is committed on one section of the society then another section remains silent; if it is a problem for the students, others remain silent; if it is a cruelty against the Dalits, others passively witness it; how very dangerous this opportunist approach is! Is it not essential for all democratic forces to rally together whenever human rights are being violated?

Law college students said that they were attacked by the police because they staged agitations condemning the fee hike and increase in the price of essential commodities, and they supported the total bandh called by the opposition parties. As a result, some people even debate if students need politics? Are fee and price hikes unrelated to the students? Are not the students affected because of that? If students take part in such protests, must political overtones be given to it? A judicial inquiry has been ordered regarding this attack on the students. Any single commission that inquired into the police atrocities has never shown the proceedings of the police to be guilty! Will the report of this judicial commission report alone be any exception?

Police force is an instrument of extremely horrid terrorism structured by the state! So, armed state agencies like the police are being renovated and sharpened with more intelligence facilities! Because it is used as state terrorism's tool for oppression, the authoritarian arrogance of the police has increased. In this situation, the revamping of the police institution is a necessity in our times. If weapons are heaped in excess with a department filled with all irregularities such as corruption, bribery, wrongdoings . . . what else will happen? Where will human rights and democracy be?

At least now the upholders of democracy must think about the essential need for entirely restructuring the police institution! Awareness on human rights must be made as a fundamental education for the police. The police organization must be structured such that party politics cannot interfere in it.

Otherwise, what will happen to the position of the subaltern people if the police and judicial institutions lie at the feet of party politics? The ruling gang will always support state terrorism. It is the duty of the proletariat to kick it out and break it down! What is real terrorism? Who is a terrorist? America says it is Bin Laden! Rouse— not a student, but a commoner over there—and ask him, 'Who is a terrorist?'... He will point towards the police!

26 DECEMBER 2001

Notes

1. On the night of 7 December 2001, the Tamil Nadu police descended on the Government Law College hostel at Chennai and brutally attacked the students. In a gross violation of Supreme Court orders, the police force ordered the arrest and detention of students.
2. The National Human Rights Commission has noted that in the one year the period ending March 2002, it has received as many as 1308 complaints of custodial death.
3. Kalpana Sumathi, a private school teacher at the Thalli village in Dharmapuri district was taken to the police station where she was locked up in a storeroom,

beaten up, four policemen raped her one after the other, and they attempted to murder her. When she fell unconscious she was dumped in a ditch. This custodial rape took place in 1988. A Sessions Court at Krishnagiri convicted four policemen (three constables Govindan, Govidasamy, Selvaraj and one inspector, Balasubramaniam) and sentenced them to eight years rigorous imprisonment (RI)—while the minimum imprisonment for rape is a ten-year RI. In the appeal of the four police personnel in the Madras High Court against their conviction and sentence, their defence counsel put forth an outrageous argument that Kalpana Sumathi had falsely implicated the policemen in order to get a job and compensation.

4. On 2 June 1992, Padmini, a Dalit woman who worked as a sweeper in an educational institution in Chidambaram, was picked up by the Annamalai Nagar police, in order to extort a confession from her husband, Nandagopal, an university employee, who was in illegal police detention because of being arrested on 29 May 1992. His arrest was not accounted for. On the day she was picked up by the police, Padmini was gang-raped by five policemen at the Annamalai Nagar police station. She was also stripped and tortured in front of her husband. Her husband Nandagopal was 'found' hanging on 3 June 1992, though he actually died following four days of torture. The postmortem report on his body showed twenty-one injuries related to torture. The policemen indulged in framing records to escape from the crime of custodial death. Padmini was picturized by the ruling party as being a 'loose' woman of 'low' character.

5. On 29 July 1993, Vijaya, a tribal woman of the Athiyur village in the Pondicherry state was arrested and raped by five policemen. To further harass Vijaya and to clear themselves from the crime, the policemen linked her with a petty theft case, although she was innocent and had no connection with that occurence. One month later, a fact-finding team of eight people inquired into the incident. On 7 February 1994, a revenue official of the Villupuram district issued an announcement that Athiyur Vijaya was indeed raped by the police. Following this, Prof. Kalvimani appealed to the National Human Rights Commission which directed the Madras High Court in 1997 to inquire into this incident and submit a report. The judge who conducted inquiries into this, also confirmed that Vijaya had been raped by the police and he suggested that a sum of Rs.50,000 be given to her from the Pondicherry Chief Minister's Relief Fund. That money was never given to her. Under the SC/ST (Prevention of) Atrocities Act, the inquiry must have been completed within three months, and Vijaya must have been given a sum of Rs.1000 per month or a permanent job. But even ten

years after the incident, Vijaya has received no compensation and continues to battle for justice.

6. Though section 160 of the Criminal Procedure Code prohibits police conducting inquiries from questioning female witnesses at any place other than their residences; violations of this are very common. In 1995, Rangamma of the Orthanadu village testified that she was picked up from her house and forcibly taken to the police station under the guise of being questioned. (Police visits to her home were not a new thing, because her husband had been repeatedly arrested.) At the police station she was raped again and again by three policemen; she therefore lost consciousness. In the morning she was allowed to go home with the warning that she should not reveal anything.

7. Policemen who spotted the Dalit woman, Indira Gandhi, and her lover at the Anna bus stand in Madurai, took them for an interrogation to the police station, and raped her. The Viduthalai Chiruthaigal put up posters all over the city condemning the horrific nature of the police towards women, and as a consequence, the concerned policemen were dismissed from service.

8. In October 2001, Rita Mary of Tiruvottriyur was gang-raped by police personnel while she was in custody in the Gingee sub-jail. A police inspector Sandhanapandian kidnapped Rita who had come to the Aathur bus-stand, he took her to the police station where she was gang-raped by the policemen. Later, the policeman sold her to pimps. Also, cases of prostitution was filed against Rita. Responding to the queries raised by Thirumaavalavan in the Legislative Assembly on 13 March 2002 regarding this police atrocity, the Chief Minister announced on 15 March 2002 that Rita would be given a compensation of Rs.5,00,000 and she would be allotted a Housing Board home.

9. For details about the police terrorism at Kodiyankulam, see note no.11, pp. 9-10.

10. The Gomathinayagam Commission of inquiry which probed into the police atrocities against the Dalits at Kodiyankulam in 1995 ended up submitting a report that was entirely anti-democratic, anti-Dalit and anti-social justice. The politically motivated report favored the ADMK the party that was in power during the police atrocity and it absolved the dominant Thevar caste group of all responsibility for the violence against the Dalits. In order to protest against the findings of this panel, the Viduthalai Chiruthaigal launched a statewide agitation programme and copies of the report were set afire in front of the District Collectorates of

Chennai, Madurai, Sivagangai, Theni, Virudhunagar, Tiruchirapalli, Karur and Perambalur on 10 December 1999, coinciding with the Human Rights Day. (See also photograph on p.78)

11. For details about the brutality of the police that made a graveyard of the Gundupatti village, see note no.12, p.10.

12. In one of the severely horrifying instances of the increasingly anti-Dalit character of the state apparatus, the Tamil Nadu police opened fire on a pro-Dalit rally that took place on 23 July 1999 in the southern district of Tirunelveli that left seventeen people, including women and an one-year old infant, Vignesh, dead. The toll is actually many times higher, for, this count has been arrived at by taking into account only the number of bodies retrieved. Since most of the bodies were retrieved many days after the incident, the police force (responsible for the deaths) performed the last rites.

The rally organized jointly by the Tamil Manila Congress, a breakaway faction of the Tamil Nadu Congress Committee (that has since merged) and the Puthiya Tamizhagam, a Dalit party, to voice the demands of the Manjolai estate workers turned tragic when the police force brutally opened fire and lathi-charged the peaceful rallyists. The police not only assaulted and grievously wounded those participating in the rally, but also blocked all escape routes except the Thamarabharani River. Even those who struggled to swim to safety were violently assaulted by the police.

Background: The labourers working in the Manjolai tea estate had been working as bonded labourers, for extremely long hours and they were paid very paltry wages. Therefore this rally had been organized to put forth the demand to free the bonded labourers and with the request to the Government to take over the estate to ensure that the workers were treated properly. The estate workers had peacefully agitated and staged a dharna on 9 July 1999 before the office of the District Collector. Then, 652 estate workers, including 198 women had been arrested and imprisoned in the Tiruchi Prison, which is hundreds of kilometres away from the Tirunelveli district.

So this rally was planned and taken on 23 July 1999, demanding among other things, the release of the imprisoned workers. In this rally prominent leaders of the opposition parties participated which included seven Members of Legislative Assembly.

13. A one-man Commission of Inquiry by Justice Mohan was appointed by the State Government of Tamil Nadu to probe into the ghastly episode of police atrocities that took place in a rally held on 23 July 1999 in the

Tirunelveli district, which left seventeen people dead (see above note no.12). The blatantly biased report of the inquiry commission reads: 'The police attack on those who had come to participate in the rally was inevitable. The death of the eleven people who had fallen into the river is only an accident; the police did not beat them while they were swimming in the river. The rest of them—six people died because they got into the river with their injuries and swam. (Even for that, the police are not responsible.)'

The Commission Report was openly predisposed, and it only quoted selective lines from news items that were anti-Dalit. The Commission accepted the police version of the video as evidence. Every other version, filmed by television channels and independent camerapersons, was ignored and not included as evidence. He also went on to record that people jumped into the river only because the rally turned unruly, and he completely absolved the role of the police in this tragedy. The Mohan Commission also put forth the irrational recommendation that henceforth all political rallies must be banned in the state.

14. After the ADMK led by Jayalalitha captured power in May 2001, the DMK took a procession on 12 August 2001 to condemn the arrest of its leaders. The police indulged in lathi-charging and opened fire at the rallyists and five people were killed. According to newsreports, over hundred volunteers of the DMK and twelve journalists were injured, a few of them grievously.

15. The Coimbatore police force, in collusion with the Hindu Munnani (a fundamentalist organization affiliated to the Sangh Parivar) unleashed planned terror on the Muslims for three days, 29 November to 1 December 1998. The unprecedented communal conflagration that reportedly caused loss of property worth two hundred crores, left twenty Muslim youth and three Hindus dead. The murder of Selvaraj, a police constable, was the immediate event that sparked off the riots, which was, nevertheless highly-organized, with the Hindu Munnani and the police force joining together to target the Muslims. They set fire to Muslim shops, smashed pavement carts and opened fire on the Muslims. When the Muslim youth injured in the police firing where brought to the hospital, they were stabbed or lynched to death. Petrol was poured on the victims and they were set afire at the hospital itself. Even a twelve-year-old Muslim boy, who was brought to the hospital for a severe hand-injury was killed.

16. In the worst prison tragedy that rocked post-independent India, nine prisoners and a jailer were killed and 128 others injured in rioting and arson and subsequent police firing in the high security Chennai Central

Prison on 17 November 1999. The rioting by the inmates broke out following the 'mysterious' death of 'Boxer' Vadivelu, a detainee who died after being admitted to the Government General Hospital. Vadivelu is reported to have been popular among the detainees because he fought for their rights and refused to pay bribes to the jail authorities. People's Union for Civil Liberties (PUCL) which inquired into this incident, found that the Deputy Jailer Jayakumar was known for his skill in torturing prisoners who were removed to quarantine—where they were stripped naked and kicked by the warders. Vadivelu who often ran into skirmishes with Jayakumar was quarantined and tortured from 12-15 November. He was taken to the General Hospital on 16 November. When news of his death reached the prisoners they had become restive. At the rollcall they demanded an explanation for his death, but the explanation did not convince them. The prisoners were attacked by the warders with lathis and rods. The prisoners burnt the Deputy Jailer Jayakumar, and the records room was set afire. This led to full-scale rioting, anti-riot police forces were called in. According to PUCL reports, it was in the subsequent police firing that nine inmates lost their lives, and over 120 of them were injured.

17. Human rights and civil liberties groups in the states of Tamil Nadu, Karnataka and Kerala have often raised protests against the STF's Veerappan hunt operations that cause excessive and unrecountable damages to the tribals inhabiting these forests. Predominantly, the victims of these atrocities have been women. In fact, when a one-man Commission of Inquiry by Justice Sadasivam was appointed to look into the atrocities committed by the STF and to suggest compensation measures, many tribals feared to depose before the committing citing fear of retaliation. Newsreports reveal that over 90 people have been arrested and shot dead, more than 60 tribal women have been raped or molested and about 300 people have been detained and tortured. Totally 124 people were detained under the Terrorist and Disruptive Activities (Prevention) Act (TADA) for eight to nine years. Of these, the High Court convinced of their innocence acquitted 109 persons.

18. Sankaralingapuram village comes under the general constituency of Sankaralingapuram Panchayat in Vilathikulam limits in the Tuticorin district. Because Dalits had not been provided with any basic amenities despite their repeated demands for several years to the village Panchayat, they decided to field their own candidate in the Panchayat elections. So, when Panchayat elections were announced, Vijayan, a Dalit from the nearby Challisettipatti village was persuaded to file a nomination for the Panchayat

President post. The oppressor caste Naidus were infuriated and they attacked Ponraj, a brother-in-law of Vijayan, and his friend Raju, who were busy campaigning on 17 October 2001, a day prior to the elections. They were seriously injured and had to be hospitalized.

On the election day, polling booths were setup both in the Naidu and Dalit areas of the village. When the Dalits in the Naidu area of the village ventured to vote, they were prevented from casting their votes and insulted by their caste names. This led to a quarrel and when it was reported to the police, they rushed to the polling booth setup near the cheri and attacked the Dalits. The Naidu candidate went on to win the elections. Later clashes between the Dalits and the oppressor castes continued, but the police only arrested the Dalits.

The Dalits staged a road-roko at the Sankaralingapuram bus stop on 16 November 2001 in order to bring the caste-discriminatory attitude of Pudur police to the notice of the higher-ranking officials and to the Government. Pudur police officials, led by the inspector descended on the scene and immediately resorted to a lathi-charge, without any provocation. As the protestors scattered, a few policemen caught hold of a Dalit boy, Manickam (19) and brutally beat him up. Dalits ran to the rescue of the boy and it incensed the police who started pelting stones on the Dalits. This ensued in a melee of sorts, and the Dalits retaliated. During this time, a police constable, Murugan, who got down from a bus (and was in mufti) joined in the attack. The police opened fire on the Dalits, sending them running back to the cheri. At 10:00 a.m. that day, a police battalion entered the Sankaralingapuram cheri and launched a motivated attack on the Dalits, destroyed property worth tens of lakhs. Several Dalit women were taken captive and arrested. The arrested Dalits were then taken to the police station where they were harassed, abused and savagely beaten-up. There, they heard that the police constable Murugan had died of the injuries at the police lathi-charge.

More than 160 persons including women and children were arrested. Of the arrested, 66 women, around ten infants and children were remanded to judicial custody in the Tiruchi Central Prison and 52 men were taken to the Palayamkottai Prison. Some of the very young children who were lodged in the prison included: Shobana (2), Parameshwari (5), Bharati (4), Amalan (2), Vinithan (2), Tiresh (4), Akash (1), William (4), Carole (1), Christopher (5), Selva (3), Abhishek (4), Subhashini (2), Priyadharshini (five months), Vinodhini (five months), Selvam (nine months), Sebishti (four months). About ten Dalit schoolchildren were lodged in the

Palayamkottai Juvenile home. An eighth-standard student, Ramamurthy, who was the twenty-third accused in the murder of policeconstable Murugan was booked under the IPC sections 147, 302, 307, 332, 341. Everybody had fled the cheri and only ten women had stayed behind. Tension surrounded the village after the police attack, and police barred entry to the village.

On 3 December 2001, when Thirumaavalavan with thousands of his supporters tried to enter the village, he was stopped by the police at Pudur itself. After talks with the police, they allowed only three cars of Thirumaavalavan to enter the village. On the road from Pudur to Sankaralingapuram, hundreds of police personnel lined the streets. At the entrance of Sankaralingapuram, they were blocked by the Additional Superintendent of Police who prevented their entry. After much persuasion Thirumaavalavan and his supporters entered the cheri, they were the first to enter it. From outside, Sankaralingapuram looked as though nothing had befallen it because, the police had changed their tactics. Unlike other places of atrocities, they had not spoilt the roofs of the houses, all the looting, plundering and pillaging was restricted to the insides of Dalit homes. With the exception of eight men, all the 140 Dalits who had been arrested were released after 70 days. On 15 March 2002, in the State Legislative Assembly, Thirumaavalavan demanded action and inquiry into the Sankaralingapuram police atrocity. The Chief Minister in her response informed the Assembly that the District Collector had been asked to furnish a report on the matter within thirty days. A Joint Coordination Committee headed by Dalit organizations, communist parties, and human rights groups was formed and they conducted a public hearing into the incident on 16 and 17 March. On 30 March 2002, the Chief Minister Jayalalitha visited the Sankaralingapuram village and dispensed a relief amount of Rs.13,33,700 rupees towards damage of property, though the actual loss was much higher.

m.a.l.e d.o.m.i.n.a.t.i.o.n

KANNAGI*
A Symbol of Militancy

Only men have been involved, right from the creation of the Kannagi epic, to the carving of her statue from a rock brought from the Himalayas, to building a shrine in her memory, to the erection of the statue on the Marina Beach during the Second World Tamil Conference in 1968, and, now, to demanding that her statue be reinstalled at the same place! It appears that then and now, any woman has not supported this woman! In this situation,

---

* Kannagi, is the heroine of the ancient Tamil epic *Silappadhikaram* (lit. Tale of the Anklet). Her husband, Kovalan, of Poompuhar deserts her, seeking the love of a courtesan, Madhavi. He later returns to Kannagi, who forgives him. She gave him her anklet, to sell to raise money and they migrated to Madurai city. He is implicated falsely and executed for stealing the Pandya queen's anklet (filled with pearls) that resembled Kannagi's (filled with rubies). An enraged Kannagi challenges the Pandya king, he dies on realizing the mistake. She rails against the gods for their injustice and in her fury, Madurai is devoured by fire.

when a woman's statue has been removed by another woman,[1] it is necessary to observe the reaction and the impact that has been created among women.

Kannagi is only the whip often cracked in frenzy by men who oppress and repress women and confine them to the kitchen. Kannagi is the bridle rope used for ages and ages by the weakling men against women. Kannagi is the protective fortress of the hegemonic mindset of men who say that they can live in any manner, but the wife alone must live according to their word. If a statue must be erected for such a Kannagi, there remains a silent question mark. How will women open their mouths regarding the removal of the Kannagi statue? Any women's organization has not taken this up! Because the reason is that Kannagi is more a symbol of male domination than a symbol of chastity! So, how can women be expected to come forward to retain and protect such a symbol!

Under these circumstances, it is necessary to know what women really feel about characters like Kannagi and Nalayini that men have upheld and established. When it is being taught, 'Only if women live like them, they are chaste! Otherwise they are unchaste!' how can women today frankly criticize them? Will not those who criticize like this be blemished? In that manner, if they are not criticizing the stories of Kannagi, Nalayini, etc., fearing blemish, can it be considered that today's women approve of it? While the husbands are Kovalans wandering in search of Madhavis, to be unquestioning and dumb like Kannagi—is this the definition of chastity? Carrying one's husband, who is oozing with wounds and suffering from skin disease, in a basket and dropping him in the prostitute's home, like Nalayini did—is it the identity of chastity to endorse impropriety? So the stories of Kannagi and Nalayini are only in order to make women approve of the course of establishing the male domination by justifying the impropriety of men. Thus, chastity is only a violence fabricated by men—for the benefit of men—and imposed on women. Tamil society's code of life has been ordered only central to that.

The Chera, Chola and Pandya Kings in that period were very supportive of that. For instance, Raja Raja Cholan[2] planned and developed the devadasi system[3] where a few specific women were dedicated ritually and made to dance in temples. It is because of the importance the king gave to the one-sided code of chastity that was imposed on women. That is, without the capacity to control the impropriety of men, and at the same time, with the male dominative mindset of protecting the chastity thrust on women alone; by making specific women into dasis, the Chola king ruined their chastity. So, to ensure basically that 'the impropriety of men must not be restrained, but women's chastity must also not be spoilt' that king created the community of dasis. In the same manner, giving importance to chastity, the Chera king Senguttuvan and his brother Ilango Adigal have competitively upheld Kannagi.[4]

Customs and proverbs prevailing among the people serve as evidence that such a habit of imposing one-sided chastity was not formed yesterday or today, but it has been in practice for ages.

Kal aanaalum kanavan! Pul aanaalum purusan! Kanavane kankanda daivam (lit. even if he is a stone, he is the husband/even if he is grass, he is the husband/the husband himself is the god) Such proverbs compel that no matter whatever kind of person the husband is, the women alone have to be faithful.

It is being said that only this proverb, *Kallane aanalum Kanavan! Pullane aanalum Purusan!* (lit. even if he is thief, he is the husband/ even if he a cheat, he is the husband) has metamorphosed into the above saying. So, this means that even if the husband is a thief, even if he is mean, the wife has to be bound by him and be chaste.

The formation of the idea that women alone must not lose chastity was born out of the men's love for ownership. It is possible to comprehend that because of a man's wish that his property must only reach his heir, the cultures like marriage and chastity were defined. In the ancient communitarian society where concepts like family, property, etc., had not taken shape; the rules of chastity had not sprung. Contrarily, only after the feeling—'My home, my garden'—of ownership of property formed, he starts to plan to whom it must reach after him. As a result, he deems that after his death, his property must only be for his true heir. Therefore, the necessity to establish his paternity of the child is created for him.

Consequently only marriage and chastity, etc., were created. So he holds the ritual of marriage by publicly making a woman into his wife, only to establish that the heir obtained through her is his. That way, even though he marries publicly, chastity was imposed on women to establish that the child born to her was only of him. So only the materialist desire of men has created the ritual called marriage and the fiction called chastity!

Symbols of chastity like Kannagi and Nalayini are only symbols of male domination! So, to retain and protect such symbols, how can the support of today's women be expected? Even then, the symbol of Kannagi is needed! Not because she is a symbol of chastity, but because she is a symbol of militancy for she protected justice by directly pointing out to the sceptred king himself that he was a murderer!

16 January 2002

Notes

1. The Kannagi statute on the Marina Beach was removed by the Jayalalitha Government because of an alleged road accident. It also ruled out its reinstallation citing traffic inconvenience.
2. Raja Raja Cholan was a great king of the later Chola dynasty who ruled from 985 A.D. to 1014 A.D. He established the highly famous and tallest Peruvudaiyar (the name has been Sanskritized: Brihadeeswarar) temple in Tanjore in Tamil Nadu. It was during his reign that the devadasi system was established. He appointed 400 women dancers to this temple and each of them were given a residence and about seven acres of land. These women were called *pathi ilaar* (lit. those without husbands). They lived as a community outside the village and were called *Thalicheri Pendugal* (lit. glamorous and blooming young women). This is an inscription in the temple built by him.
3. The devadasi (lit. maidservants of god) system refers to the heinous practice of ritually dedicating women as dancing girls to temples. These women were made into victims of the worst kind of sexual oppression, they were forced to satiate the 'desires' of Brahmin priests and members of the royalty. This misery reached its peak under state patronage and it subsequently degenerated until it was banned by an act of law.
4. Ilango Adigal was the brother of the Chera king Senguttuvan. He composed the *Silappadhikaram*.

b.i.a.s

ARE YOU THE GANDHIAN MONKEYS ?

After the dates were fixed for holding the by-election for the vacant seats in the three Legislative Assembly constituencies: Andipatti, Saidapet and Vaniyambadi, all the parties scrutinized the old ties within a span of six months and were strategically planning the formation of new fronts, the Election Commission's sudden announcement came as a shock not only for the opposition parties, but for everybody; there can be no different opinion on that! The reason for the shock is the announcement of the Election Commission that at present the elections would be postponed in the constituencies of Saidapet and Vaniyambadi because of malpractices in the inclusion of new voters, and that elections would proceed as planned in the constituency of Andipatti alone, because such malpractices did not take place there.

'Without malpractices, there are no elections'—is the Indian electoral political history! Elections have not taken place in which 'wheeling and dealing' has not taken place before and after the polling! Elections could be defined as 'wheeling and dealing' to that extent its history is full of the evidential scars of malpractices, violence, defrauding, etc.

Only to avoid such frauds and malpractices, new efforts like electronic voting machines and voter identity cards are being adopted. Even in this, new malpractices are showing up. If one calculates the crores of money that the Indian Government has poured for these electoral exercises that are the complete form of such malpractices, one's heart is surging! Let this be on one side!

Postponing elections—which are the source of malpractices—by laying the blame on malpractices, reveals that another malpractice has taken place. It is not surprising when the opposition parties make noises that in this malpractice which has taken place behind the screens there is the interference of Tamil Nadu's ruling party. The appeal of the opposition parties that election must be held in all the three constituencies, otherwise all types of malpractices will take place in Andipatti, is not without justice.[1] In the protection of democracy, even more than the concern of the ruling party, the opposition parties have greater responsibility.

In that manner, the interest shown by the opposition parties in the by-election is worthy of praise! But the same frenzy and concern has not gushed forth to even stress that elections be held in the Panchayat constituencies reserved for the subordinated Dalits! Why is that? Whether the ruling party or the opposition party, in the problems related to the Dalits alone, are they all in the same team? The team of monkeys visualized by Gandhi? Even if the eyes see and the ears hear, the mouth alone is never opened at any point of time! What is the name for this? Democracy? Casteocracy?

When it was not possible to hold elections for the past five years and more, how did the administration take place in these Panchayats? This is not a matter of surprise for those who remained without elections for a long period of time because they did not want to grant reservation for the Dalits in the Panchayat governance. What is going to be surprising for those who joined together and removed all their party flags because they wanted to ensure that a Dalit man's flag must not fly in a public place? Are not they the amusing people who, only to ensure that a Transportation Corporation must not be named after a Dalit fighter Veeran Sundaralingam[2], said no to even naming Transportation Corporations after Thiruvalluvar[3] and Periyar.[4]

By chance, if somehow a situation occurs tomorrow where a Dalit becomes a Chief Minister or a Prime Minister, one need not be surprised if they cackle that there is no need of elections here.

Those who have accepted reservation for the Dalits in the Legislative Assemblies and Parliament, why is it not possible for them to accept reservation in Panchayat administrations? Is it because the agitations appearing in the Panchayat administration will shake the foundations of the casteist social structure?

Only the *Panchayati Raj* and *Nagar Palika* Acts implemented during Rajiv Gandhi's period paved the way for reservation for women and Dalits in Panchayat administrations.[5] On that basis, only in 1996 for the first time Dalits and women came into power in the Panchayat administrations. Even then, the truth is that they are being treated as *thalaiyatti bommai* (lit. nodding dolls) who simply raise their hands for referendums. Even if the women contest and win, the husband of the elected woman, introduces himself as the Panchayat President or Vice-President or Municipality Chairman or Mayor without any embarrassment. Press them a little and ask, only then they will admit, 'It is my wife who is the President.'

On that basis only, in the majority of the places where the Dalits have won, the persons elected as the Vice-President, unjustly annex and rule as Presidents.

Apart from this, what a great shame it is when they prohibit Dalits from contesting in elections. Why do the opposition parties not consider this at least as a loss of face?

During the five-year period of the last DMK Government's rule, the Tamil Nadu Election Commission said that even though six announcements were done for holding the elections, no one came forward to file their nomination papers. Currently the same situation is continuing in the Panchayat elections in the ADMK rule too! In the Panchayat constituencies of Pappapatti, Keeripatti, Nattarmangalam and Kottakatchiyendhal near Madurai, why has no one come forward to contest?[6] The officialdom is diverting the problem by saying that the reason is not any threat based on casteist hatred.

If the authorities and the ruling parties only don't have concern, is it like that even for the opposition parties? Any party has not shown a least bit of concern in fielding nominees in those constituencies. In these specified constituencies, was there not a Dalit in at least one party? If the parties of those who apprehend that the interference of the Dalit parties changes the problem into caste clash are open to all, then a solution can be found without the occurrence of any caste-clash.

In approaching the problems of the Dalits there is no difference even between the Dravidian parties and the Communist parties!

The Central Command of the Viduthalai Chiruthaigal has decided to boycott the by-election in order to expose all the parties; to condemn the ruling party and the Election Commission; and to insist on immediately holding elections in the above mentioned reserved Panchayat constituencies.

Even if the saying *Therdhal Paadhai, Thirudar Paadhai* (lit. the path of election, is the path of thieves) is truth; when that alone is in practice, it is the people's path to protect the democracy of the majority of the working class even there. That is why, instead of taking benefit alone as a yardstick in the electoral path, the Viduthalai Chiruthaigal has decided to boycott the by-election.

Political parties! You be in any front of your choice in electoral politics! When it comes to the problems of the Dalits, bravely dare to say whose side you are on!

30 January 2002

Notes

1. Andipatti was the constituency from which the current Chief Minister of Tamil Nadu, Jayalalitha, contested and was elected. It was alleged that this is the main reason why there was disparity in the procedures of the Election Commission.
2. A Dalit hero who served as the commander of the army of the Naicker king, Veerapandiya Kattabomman. The decision to create a new transport corporation in his name in the Virudhunagar district was announced in April 1997, and this decision caused a fresh cycle of violence in the southern districts of Tamil Nadu. The dominant oppressor castes in these districts, the Thevars, opposed this proposal, threw stones and vandalized the buses and refused to ride them.
3. Ancient Tamil poet and author of the *Thirukkural*, a famous and classic Tamil literary composition.
4. Transport Corporations in Tamil Nadu carried the names of Periyar, Thiruvalluvar, Rajiv Gandhi, etc. This decision to remove names of individuals from Transport Corporations was actually a recommendation of the Justice Mohan Commission of inquiry that investigated the oppressor caste attack on Dalits in the southern districts in 1997. The Government of Tamil Nadu, which was then ruled by the DMK implemented it.
5. The Seventy-Third Amendment to the Constitution of India paved the way for the establishment of Panchayati Raj. The amendment mandates that resources, responsibility and decision-making power be devolved from the Central Government and placed in the hands of the rural grassroot people, with elections to the local councils being held every five years. The late Prime Minister Rajiv Gandhi championed the rebirth of the Panchayati Raj system and in April 1993, following the passage of the Seventy-Third Amendment in 1992, it became a part of the Constitution and was inserted

therein as Article 243D. Simultaneously, the Seventy-Fourth Amendment of 1992, relating to the *Nagar Palika*, i.e. Municipalities, became Article 243T of the Constitution. In 1996, the first elections to these Panchayats and municipalities were held. The amendment had tremendous impact because it provided reservation to the most oppressed sections of society: Dalits and Women. While reservation for the Dalits was made proportional to their population, one third of all seats—including one third of all Panchayat presidencies—was reserved for women; these reserved constituencies were on a rotation basis and decided by the Election Commission.

6. Refer note no.1, pp. 28-30 about the murder of democracy taking place in these five reserved Panchayat constituencies.

e.t.h.n.i.c. i.s.s.u.e

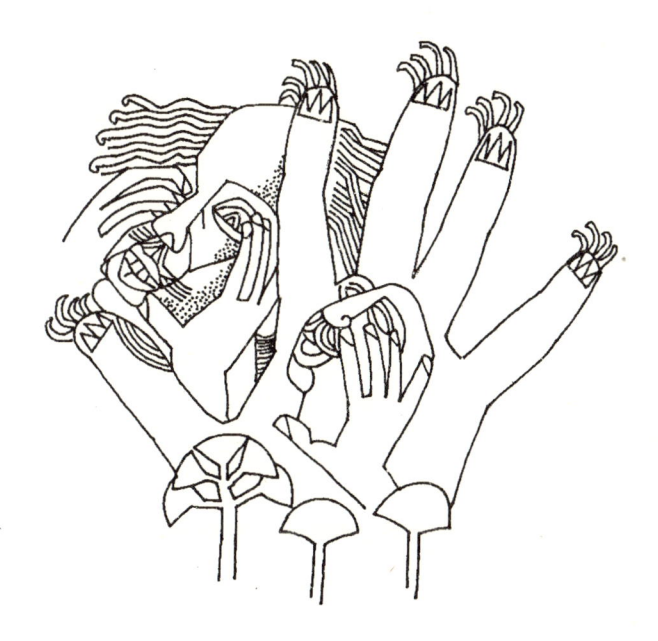

A SLAP IN
THE FACE!

All struggles are only towards talks! Whether it is an unconstitutional armed struggle or a state sanctioned people's agitation, it moves towards talks, it is natural! Only after the talks there are solutions to problems! No matter whatever the form of the struggle, appropriate talks also being held is inevitable.

In that manner, it is slightly consoling that the Eelam liberation struggle, which has been continuing for more than the last thirty years, has moved towards talks! That too, it is praiseworthy that both the sides, the Sinhalese Government and the Liberation Tigers of Tamil Eelam (LTTE), have climbed down and come closer! The basic reason for this is the political situation that has now been formed in Lanka.

Today, the new Prime Minister Ranil Wickremesinghe personally met the Buddhist monks and sought their cooperation for a solution to this problem—which is an evidence for the creation of a new political milieu in the Sri Lankan land which has been reeking of blood for the past two generations.

In these circumstances, it is amusing that a reactionary political situation—which questions: 'Can the political advisor of the LTTE Anton Balasingham stay here and hold talks with the Sinhalese Government?'—is evolving in Tamil Nadu. The Indian Government has not bragged a bit regarding this! But the Tamil Nadu Government and a few Tamil Nadu political parties are screaming here in a great panic and it appears that it will create a stumbling block not only for the talks but also for the Eelam problem itself!

When the Sinhalese Prime Minister himself has come forward to remove the economic embargo on the Tamilians, to lift the ban on the Tigers and to lend a helping hand in support of the Tamilians, what does it show when there are voices shouting in Tamil Nadu against the Tamil race? Like the Tamil poet Namakkal Kavignar wrote, *Tamizhan enroru inam undu, thaniye avarukoru kunamundu* (lit. there is a race called the Tamilians, they have a unique nature)—it reveals the unique nature of Tamilians.

What would be the distinct special nature of the Tamilians? For that, we get as a reply, the verses of Subramania Bharati's song:

Sondha sodhararkal,
Thunbaththil saadhal kandum,
Sindhai irangar adi kiliye — Nam
Semmai marandharadi.

(lit. Though their own siblings/ Died in sadness/ Oh dear, they will not feel pity/ They have forgotten our culture).

These lines of Bharati expose the unique nature of the

LTTE Supremo Velupillai Prabhakaran fielded questions for more than two hours at the International Press Meet in Killinochi on 10 April 2002 in which over six hundred reporters from around the world took part. Seated next to Prabhakaran is LTTE's political strategist Mr. Anton Balasingham and Mr. Thamil Chelvan (far left), head of the LTTE's political wing.

Tamilians and are very apt even today! The whole world knows the manner in which the lives of the Eelam Tamilians were crushed by the oppression of the Sinhalese sectarian forces!

In this situation, this screaming simply exposes that Tamil Nadu does not even have the concern that the Norwegian nation (which is not even a bit related to the Eelam Tamilians) has!

It is a slap that fell on the face of every Tamilian, that the Norwegian Government is doing the duties and the fieldwork that Tamil Nadu should have done standing at the forefront. Instead of feeling ashamed or agonized about this, the Tamilian is jumping from sky to land, 'Can the Tigers hold their talks sitting in Tamil Nadu?'

Why? It is because of the attitude that considers attachment to the Tamil language, the Tamil race and the Tamil land as 'anti-national.' To stand against the liberation of a nationality by showing a leader's assassination as the reason; is it because of affection on that leader? Or is it plain patriotism?

No one can argue that Rajiv Gandhi's assassination is the solution for a separate Eelam or that it is fair! For that brutal assassination, not one, but three inquiry commissions, special investigation teams, judgments ... it is a major crime if someone interferes and tries to save anyone from this! But is it ethical to show that adverse deed as a reason and to commit another adverse deed? Is it correct to stand against the liberation of a race itself?

A ethnic liberation struggle is not something that happens by the Tamil race alone and for Tamil Eelam alone; all over the world ethnic consciousness is spreading and rising its head. The separation of Soviet Union into several different countries is its manifestation!

Lenin had stressed that every nationality had the right of cessation along with the right of self-determination; because of that political pact the Soviet Union separated into distinct nations without damage and it flourished. Lacking such an understanding, countries like India and Sri Lanka fiercely repress national liberation struggles! The reason for this is a fascist attitude that allows no place for the opinions and feelings of others! In that manner, the Indian Government is not ready to accept the liberation of Tamil Eelam even on a policy level!

Even more than the oppression by the Sinhalese Government, the policy of the Indian Government is a major reason why the Eelam liberation struggle has been prolonged for so many years and why its liberation is at a standstill. The Indian Government considers the attainment of liberation by Eelam as a threat to its territorial integrity. Perhaps this is based on the fear that it shall be a shared aspiration and inspiration to the nationality consciousness that often explodes here and there in the Indian states. It is a reality that the Indian Government is more determined than the Sinhalese Government in refusing the liberation of Eelam.

The Indian Government which openly trained not only the Tigers, but also militants belonging to all groups, later, landed its military troops in Eelam in support of the Sinhalese President Jayawardene and against the fighters for the liberation of Eelam!

It entered forcefully even though the Tigers, the other militant groups and the people of Tamil Eelam said that they were against it. In the course of time, Premadasa who succeeded Jayawardene opposed the Indian Peace Keeping Force (IPKF) and made them quit. A Sinhalese soldier attempted to attack Rajiv Gandhi who participated in the parade—these incidents are only indications that even the Sinhalese didn't accept Indian Government's interference.

But today the Sinhalese Government and the Liberation Tigers are expecting the cooperation of the Indian Government. The political situation in Sri Lanka has changed in that manner. In this state of affairs, even before the Indian Government opens its mouth, the Tamil Nadu Government and the political parties in Tamil Nadu are declaring their opposition in fierce competition with each other.

It is not understandable whether it is against the LTTE or if it is against the people of Tamil Eelam. Is it ethical to tie-up the Rajiv Gandhi assassination and the liberation of Eelam and thereby put a stopgap? Is it correct?

If the leader of the LTTE, Prabhakaran is himself guilty no one is going to interfere in inquiring or punishing him! With the consideration that they are opposing the LTTE, they must not stand against the liberation of a nationality, right?

The revolutionary Dr. Ambedkar criticized Nehru's Panchsheel policy remarking, 'rather than giving importance to constructive nation building, the Indian Government is spending the majority of the national earnings in the name of national defence. It is because of the external affairs policy of the Indian Government.' When the world war broke out, all the countries of the world stood divided as two fronts, while the Indian Government maintained neutrality as a nonaligned nation.

Due to that, lacking the support of any superpower, there is an excessive military expenditure for India because of the panic that an attack can take place at any time. Dr. Ambedkar's criticism was that a major portion of the Indian Government's earnings is wasted because of such an external affairs policy.

Likewise even today, only a relationship lacking goodwill continues between the Indian Government and all its neighboring countries like Pakistan, China, Nepal, Bangladesh, and Sri Lanka. Because of this, on the basis of national security the Indian Government's several wasteful expenditures continue!

If the Indian Government approaches this problem by taking all this into consideration, then the way for national security and South Asian peace can be found.

If the Tamil Nadu Government and the political parties here approach this problem by realizing that saying no to the talks here is not against the Tigers, but is against the liberation of a nationality, and that it is against democracy itself—the rights of nationality and the people of Tamil Eelam will receive a new life.

13 February 2002

i.m.b.a.l.a.n.c.e

JUDGMENTS
Not to Be Corrected, but to Be Changed

If judgments like this come, how will the lay people have faith on the courts?

Recently, the Madras High Court has given the verdict in a petition that the rural students must not be offered reservation in professional courses. Comprehending that they cannot compete with the urban students, the Tamil Nadu Government had reserved 25 percent of the seats in professional courses for the rural students—that is, in Law, Medicine, Engineering, etc. Such a judgment has been delivered in a litigation that was filed challenging this.

Everybody knows the circumstances of the schools functioning in the villages today. In majority of the schools, classes are held in the shade of trees because there are not enough classrooms. Likewise, there are many schools, which do not have laboratories where practical experience in the science subjects can be obtained. As enough teachers are not there in proportion to the student population, two or three classes are combined and the students are attended to simultaneously.

In these circumstances, how can the rural school students compete with the urban students who go to schools equipped with the necessary infrastructure? That is why, reservation has been granted separately to the rural students so that they too can obtain professional education. But, how can the group which laments and raises its war flag of 'No Reservation,' tolerate this? The Madras High Court has rendered this kind of justice only in a writ petition that was filed on the instigation of such a gang. So the High Court itself has resolved that if possible the rural school students can compete with the urban students.

It is a custom for the courts, tribunals, inquiry commissions and judiciary centers here to often give such shocking judgments, announcements and reports!

Six months ago, the Salem Sessions Court gave its judgment in the Melavalavu massacre case! It has delivered the verdict that the brutal murders of seven people including Panchayat President Murugesan—for having contested and won the elections in the reserved Melavalavu Panchayat constituency, in violation of the orders, and in spite of the death threats from, the caste-fanatic gang, would not be classified as a casteist atrocity.[1]

For the first time, Dalits and women were given reservation only in the Panchayat elections of 1996. The entire nation knows that the violent rampage organized by the anti-reservation gang which could not accept this, was only a blatant casteist rampage. The nadu ('state') of the non-Dalits gave the verdict: 'Melavalavu Panchayat must not be reserved for the Dalits, even if it is reserved, no Dalit should contest from it.'

Beyond all the concepts like Tamil Nadu state, the Indian state, even today there functions a nadu ('state')—a caste supremacist outfit that implements laws based on caste traditions—in some villages in the districts of Madurai, Sivagangai and Ramanathapuram in Tamil Nadu!

It was a verdict of the nadu, that 'Even if the Indian Constitution says so; a Dalit must not become a Panchayat President; the one who violates this will be beheaded.'

The Melavalavu massacre is only a massacre that took place based on this verdict! How can a court say that such a blatant casteist atrocity is not a casteist atrocity at all?

The Venmani massacre is the barbaric massacre that shook Tamil Nadu about thirty years ago! In the east Tanjore district, when the Dalits who were farm coolies in Venmani agitated against the rampant casteism and feudalistic supremacy; forty-four of them were cruelly burnt alive by a caste-fanatic landlord who was unable to tolerate their agitation—this is the horrid Venmani carnage! The inquiry court that examined Gopalakrishna Naidu, that brutal murderer, leader of the Paddy Producers Association leader and big landlord, released him as 'Not Guilty'.[2]

Only the explanation given by the court for releasing Gopalakrishna Naidu who committed such horrid murders is very amusing and strange. It was: 'It is not possible to accept that a *mirasdar* (a big landlord) who was very highly respected in the society could have involved directly in the murders! If he had wanted, he could have sent his henchmen, chances are not there that he have been directly involved in the incident! Therefore, this court releases him.' Without any shred of evidence, and based on this conjecture, the court pronounced its judgment that day.

But after few years, the peoples' forum gave him the punishment of death penalty! 'Can the people themselves take the law in their hands? Can they mete out a punishment?'—These questions may arise! The one-sided anti-people approach of the court is the

Police are seen assaulting the rallyists who are swimming to safety. The Mohan Commission report stated: "The death of the people who had fallen into the river is only an accident; the police did not beat them while they were swimming."

reason why people themselves meted out the punishment.

Like this, not only the courts, but even the inquiry commissions, are always giving amusing–surprising–shocking reports. Till now, the majority of the commissions appointed in Tamil Nadu have only buried justice and truth. The Manjolai estate workers were beaten up and killed by the police in the Thamarabharani River, but the Mohan Commission report blatantly lied by stating, 'nothing happened like that' and 'they drowned to death because they didn't know how to swim.'

Likewise, the Gomathinayagam Commission report supported the police who plundered in Kodiyankulam by declaring that the 'Police are not guilty!'[3]

This way, all the commissions have thrown impartiality in the streets and have given reports in favor of the governing authorities. How will such judgments and reports create faith on the courts and inquiry commissions? It has come to the situation where it can be sung: 'Justice? Fairness? It is sold in the market. If you have money, it can be bought!'— if this continues, will not a volcano explode among the lay people?

When the judgments have come saying that the Melavalavu massacre is not a casteist atrocity and that there is no reservation for rural students, must not the Government immediately oppose this and file appeals? In Melavalavu the time-span for appeal has

Thirumaavalavan and cadres of the Viduthalai Chiruthaigal burning copies of the Gomathinayagam Commission report in front of the Chennai Collectorate on 10 Dec 1999 as a part of their state-wide agitation program

expired! But the Government has not showed any concern in that!

By appealing in higher courts the judgments might be corrected! But these types of judgments are not to be corrected; they are to be changed!

Those who are boycotted—those who are cruelly betrayed—are comparable to earthquakes! They will not correct the judgments; they will change them!

Not only the judgments even the nation too!

27 FEBRUARY 2002

Notes

1. This case was first tried at the Melavalavu magistrate court and subsequently transferred to the IV Additional Sessions and District Court of Madurai. Based on an appeal filed by key witnesses who apprehended a threat to their lives if the case was conducted in Madurai, the Supreme

Court permitted the transfer of the cases to the Salem Sessions Court.

The judgment of the case was given on 26 July 2001. Of the 41 people who were charge-sheeted (one of them died midway during the trial), seventeen of the accused were awarded life imprisonment. In the 124 page judgment, the judge categorically states that there is no evidence that the murderers committed their crime because of a casteist reason and therefore this massacre couldn't be considered as a casteist atrocity, and thereby it couldn't be tried under the SC/ST (Prevention of) Atrocities Act. Since the State Government of Tamil Nadu had filed the case, the affected could not approach a higher forum for appeal. Although the Viduthalai Chiruthaigal put forth an appeal to the State Government to move to an higher forum for appeal, the Government did not do so, and allowed the time-frame to lapse. As a result of this, it is easy for even the sentenced killers to be out on bail and cause even greater discord. The Melavalavu massacre was treated as a multiple murder case and tried as a criminal case and not under the Scheduled Caste/ Scheduled Tribe (Prevention of) Atrocities Act. Had it been treated as a case under the Atrocities Act, a death sentence would have been imposed on all the seventeen found guilty. The police and judiciary, who are extremely and deliberately lax when it comes to issues relating to the Dalits, arrested Ramar, the prime accused in the Melavalavu mass murder only two and half years after the gruesome incident took place.

2. Refer the article, 'Must Venmani be Fenced?,' pp.169-74 for comprehensive details about the Venmani carnage.
3. For information about the Mohan Commission which probed into the Thamarabharani tragedy see note no.13, pp.54-55. Regarding Gomathinayagam Commission that inquired into the Kodiyankulam police atrocity see note no.10, pp. 53-54.

f.a.n.a.t.i.c.i.s.m

DEMOCRACY IS THE RELIGION! HUMANISM IS THE VEDA!

Palli Thalamanaithum Koil Seikuvom* (lit. we will make all schools into temples)—the poet Subramania Bharati said! Perhaps because of that the Sangh Parivar organizations like the Rashtriya Swayamsevak Sangh (RSS) and the Vishwa Hindu Parishad (VHP) are defiant and firm in saying, 'We will demolish all the mosques and construct temples.' Following the VHP's call for action that the Ram temple in Ayodhya would be built on 15 March 2002, thousands of men and women are pouring into Ayodhya for the *kar seva*. The fire of

---

* *Palli*, the Tamil word for school, also means mosque, giving a whole new dimension to the Tamil poet Subramania Bharati's lines.

enmity, which blazed all over the nation after the centuries-old historical symbol Babri Masjid was demolished, is yet to go off! It has not yet subsided! Every year, on the sixth of December that untamed fire rages.

In this situation, again and again, do we need announcements that add fuel to the fire? When the case relating to the Ayodhya issue is in the court of inquiry, and the judgment is yet to be rendered must they suddenly set the date to set fire to the entire nation? What is the need for this hurry? Must Ayodhya be made the playing field to harvest political benefits? These are the questions of doubt which the innocent people are raising in alarm! It is seen that such type of intimidatory politics is often staged whenever by-elections or general elections take place in order to collect and consolidate the vote banks.

Saying, 'Ram was born only in Ayodhya! That too, only at the place where Babar built the mosque!'—and being adamant about 'building the temple for Ram only there' indicates that more than the devotion to Ram, there is only the frenzy for political power.

It is also mentioned that even several centuries earlier, in the same place that is called the '*Ram Janmabhoomi*,' there existed a Buddhist Vihaar. A few years ago, Mai Savita, the wife of revolutionary Dr. Ambedkar declared that such a disputed land was for the Buddhists alone and that no one else had the right to it. If that is the truth, will a Buddhist Vihaar be built there? If this argument is right, it will become necessary to demolish several Hindu temples here and erect Buddhist Vihaars and Jain temples at those places! According to historical research, it is possible to know with evidence that all the shrines built in the period when Buddhism and Jainism were reigning and flying high, were annexed and were converted into Siva or Vishnu temples.

When the worship of Siva (Saivism) and the worship of Vishnu (Vaishnavism) expanded and intensified, Jainism and Buddhism were annihilated to the extent that even the footprints of their existence didn't remain. Religion with the patronage and protection of the rulers and the regime with the support of religion are established in a manner in which they are dependent on each other. The upsurge and downslide of regimes and religions are settled only on that basis. Nowhere in the world is a rule, which is devoid of religious affinity, or a religion, which is devoid of a regime's backing. Today all the countries of Europe have governments that are associated with Christianity! All the Arabian countries are associated with Islam! Buddhism is the state religion in many of the Asian countries.

In the South Asian countries, Nepal is the only country whose state religion is Hinduism! But, internationally India alone is a secular state according to its Constitution! This is the special feature of the Indian Constitution! Perhaps, because the revolutionary Dr. Ambedkar declared in the Constitution that the Indian Government shall function as a 'Secular State' instead of declaring 'Hinduism is the State religion'; his death anniversary sixth of December was chosen to demolish the Babri Masjid. Further, efforts are being taken in the name of Constitutional review to change such a Constitution. Only those who want the Indian state to be authoritatively declared as a Hindu state are centralizing power and authority and feeding communalism! For communal hatred, casteist oppression, for everything—the basic reason is only political power! The one who is anxious to capture such power, and the one who is anxious to retain it, stand in support of religion and caste! That is why, no matter how many invasions take place, how many governments change, it is unable to shake even the rootlets of caste and religion!

Even if religions like Jainism, Buddhism, Christianity, and Islam come alternately sans decline and with vigour, religion has not been abolished at any point of time! Because, religion is central to political power. That is why, the dwelling place of god (as shown by religion) and the place of dwelling of the king who rules the land is called *Koil*. The place where the king sleeps and the place where the Lord sleeps is called *Palliyarai*. So whether we say *Arasan* (lit. the ruler, king) or *Andavan* (lit. the one who ruled, presiding deity) or *Mannan* (lit. king) or *Iraivan* (lit. god, presiding male deity), they are all identities of political power.

So, all the battles that take place in the name of religion, in the name of god, are all fundamentally only battles for dominance! There is no devoutness or purity in that! But attributing purity to it and sacrificing innocent people is a treachery! Millions of people live as orphans amidst gutters on roadside pavements and poromboke lands with no hut for sitting in and no gruel to drink. Instead of guiding these people towards development or showing interest in building homes for them, is it not a mockery that they are building a temple for Ram?

The idea behind building temples in the name of god, and waging holy wars is only a dictatorial tradition of the manner of monarchy. Contrarily, when ideas in the democratic tradition of a people's rule prevail, such oppressive casteist and communalist activities will be quelled! When democracy and power reach every individual here, no violence will erupt in the name of holiness, in the name of god.

The residence and dwelling place of the god, the sanctum sanctorum of a temple or mosque or church is only a centre of power. In that way, if one is getting the grace of god, then it must also come to mean that one is getting the power and democracy! So, it means that if everyone must receive the grace of god, everyone must also get power and democracy! On that basis, communalist forces must understand and realize that the service of people by the spread of democracy is the service of god! They must realize that removing Jain temples, Buddhist Vihaars and mosques and erecting temples there, is not the service of god.

Democracy is a fundamental right whether one is Hindu or Muslim. What is a religion for, if it denies that democracy to those who belong to another religion? Religions are fabricated by men and are not created by god!

Democracy is the great religion guiding humanity! Humanism is the veda that makes the world live! Everything else that denies this is a destruction of humanity. So if there is no democracy for an individual, we shall destroy the religions.

13 MARCH 2002

n.i.g.h.t.m.a.r.e

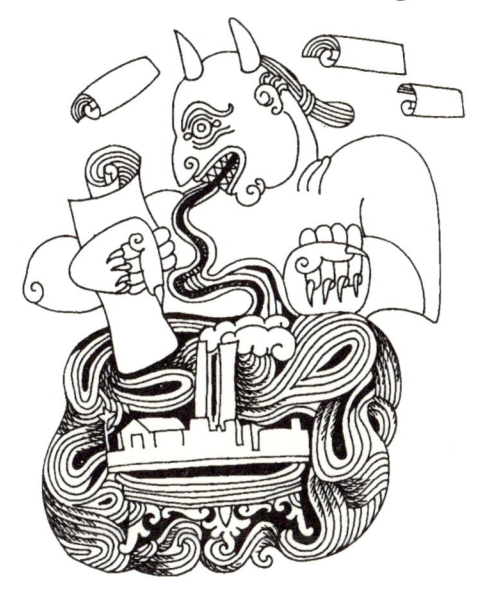

DREAMS—IMAGINATIONS—PAPERS

At that time, as an opposition party, the ADMK coordinated all the parties against the privatization of the Salem Steel Plant and vehemently raised its voice of rebellion. It presents a great shock today, for, having becoming a ruling party, in direct opposition to its earlier conduct, it supports and upholds the same privatization policy and has dared to implement it without even a little hesitation! Is it not a great betrayal to the people, to take one stand as the opposition party and to take another stand as the ruling party, in the same problem? In the Governor's speech delivered on 9 March 2002 in the Tamil Nadu Legislative Assembly, the ADMK has announced that gradually it will privatize the transportation sector. At that time, the ADMK expressed its opposition to the privatization of the Salem Steel Plant, which was under the control of the Central Government; today, on what basis does it announce that the Tamil Nadu State

Transportation Department, which is under its control, shall be gradually privatized?

Then, was the all-party demonstration in Salem held against the privatization policy? Or was it against the DMK that was part of the Central Government? If it is the principle of the ADMK to oppose the privatization policy, can it announce today, 'We will privatize the transportation sector?' The Tamil Nadu Government is providing the excuse that it is necessary to privatize the transportation sector because it is functioning at a great loss. Even for a Government that has all types of facilities, opportunities and powers, it is not possible to run a sector efficiently. How can the private owners who are at the Government's mercy run it efficiently? Does the handing over of the public sector to a private party not expose the helplessness of the Government? Or, does it reveal the profit motive of the ruling?

Handing over the public sector to the private parties will lead to power and finance getting heaped in the same place! This will pave the way for the proletariat to be repressed and exploited more and more! The Tamil Nadu Government lays the blame on the loss in the transportation sector; but the Central Government has decided to offer the Neyveli Lignite Factory—which has no loss, and has displayed its accounts of thousand crores of profit for this year alone—to private ownerships. Hence, it can be understood that privatization of a sector is not on the basis of its profit or loss; but is only based on the profit or loss of the ruling party.

No one can deny the fact that in the public sectors the administration is in utter ruins, because corruption and bribery are rampant from top to bottom! Such corruption and administrative deterioration pave the way for privatization. If the corruption rampant in the public sector is a highway robbery that takes place in the darkness, the ongoings in the private sector is a blatant daylight robbery! The fare in private buses is three times the fare in the Government buses—is it not possible to realize from this itself whether it is a daylight robbery or not?

It is calculated that due to private sectors the produce will multiply and the profit will increase! It is not known if those in power have at any point of time taken into account that the common ordinary working people will be greatly affected as a consequent reaction! Already, because of privatization the number of the labourers working in a sector will be drastically decreased! New employment opportunities will be prevented! The social justice called reservation will be denied! As a result, those who had the opportunity to taste democracy and power bit by bit for the first time, even before they can rise their heads, they will be again avenged and stamped upon. Should the rulers not realize this?

Public sectors and governmental organizations form only 15 percent of the total; private parties own the rest. In these circumstances, reservation is implemented only in these public sectors which form 15 percent. That too, it is not implemented properly or completely. Scams are taking place in which fakes have infiltrated and obtained education and employment opportunities through reservation, and received loans, etc. Such reservation has no place in private sectors. In this situation, if the existing public sector and governmental institutions are privatized what will be the position of those who have been cheated cruelly for ages and ages? Hence, the course of privatization is an act of conspiracy against reservation and against social justice. Can the 'heroine who guarded social justice' (a title bestowed on Jayalalitha) be abetting such actions of conspiracy?

Is privatization the alternative to meeting the loss due to the transportation sector? Is it the solution? It is being said that there is a financial crisis to the extent that it is not possible to bear the loss. If that is the problem, why was the cabinet expanded? Will the expenditure reduce because of that?

The Chief Minister explained the reason for the economic crunch by responding in the Legislative Assembly that the financial crisis is not only for Tamil Nadu, it is for the Central Government also; and the nation's economy and the world economy are greatly affected to that extent. In this situation, how is the Tamil Nadu Government going to fulfil the Chief Minister's 15-point programme? How is Tamil Nadu going to transform itself as the leading state in India? The foresight of the 15-point programme is appreciable! But one has to fear if it is all just simply papers where dreams and imagination have been recorded! There is no different opinion that Tamil Nadu will be the foremost state, not only in India, but in the whole world if the Chief Minister's 15-point programme—which contains several features of security like food security, livestock security, water security, health security, livelihood security—is fulfilled. But the Tamil Nadu Government which has shown concern about livelihood security, etc., has not shown any sign of concern in the 15-point programme about the security of the right to live of the socially oppressed sections: Dalits and women. When Dalits and women are not protected against atrocities how can the nation alone be improved?

The Government, which is going to increase the securities and infrastructure facilities, by announcing in the same Governor's speech that step-by-step the transportation sector will be privatized, has pushed its specialty to the back. For the entire Governor's address it has become a stain.

The announcement of privatization in the Governor's address containing the 15-point programme was like a dead fly in a fragrant cup of cardamom tea, like a lizard in lentil curry, like beautiful hair riddled with dandruff and lice, like a tasty mango infested with bugs. So, it is amusing that privatization, which is against the oppressed, is an alternative to the losses and the decline of the public sectors!

Presenting 'low-priced liquor' as an alternative to abolishing illicit liquor and preventing its ills, and presenting privatization as an alternative to the losses in the public sector, reveals the uselessness of the Government! If the alternative to illicit arrack is 'low-priced liquor', to protect people from addictive drugs like ganja, can 'low-priced ganja' be sold? Raja Raja Cholan introduced the devadasi system to protect family women from prostitution. In that manner, today, can the devadasi system be placed as an alternative to prostitution? Instead, evils must be opposed with an iron fist; to present another evil as an alternative is a great treachery to the people! Privatization too is like that!

27 March 2002

r.a.t.i.o

MAJORITY ONLY FOR DEMOCRACY AND EQUALITY

On the basis of majority alone, success or defeat is decided. In the manner of maximum numbers, more than half the total is accepted as majority. To be bound by that majority and to cooperate with it is alone considered as democracy. Based on that the Prevention of Terrorism Act (POTA) has been passed in a joint sitting of both the houses of the Parliament—the Lok Sabha and the Rajya Sabha.

Till now, in the political history of the Indian Parliament this joint sitting has been organized only two times; has again been called only now. Before this, it had been convened to pass the Dowry

Abolition Act and relating to the nationalization of banks. Currently, it was convened for the POTA, which was passed on the basis of 'majority' even though it was against the wishes of the majority of the people. This law has been passed against the opinion of the Indian National Congress which rules the majority of the Indian states, and at the same time, in support of the wishes of the BJP that rules only the single state of Gujarat.

Still, it has to be accepted that the law has been passed, on the majority basis as per the Constitution. What happens to the position of the minorities if such a political majority is established on the basis of religion or language or caste or race? Specifically, what does the terrifying declaration of the RSS, 'The minorities can live safely only in the mercy of the majority,' show? Is it democracy if the majority rules by intimidating the minorities? What happens to the nation? What happens to democracy? If it is said that the protection of democracy is in the protection of the minorities, then, to consider that such protection is only at the mercy of the majority, will only pave the way for the majority's tyranny!

So to intimidate by saying that the minority must always be dependent on the mercy of the majority, only means that the Constitution itself—which emphasizes, 'all are equal'—is being disrespected. Here, when the Constitution merely governs in name, and the Manu Dharma laws are actively ruling all the proceedings, it is not shocking that such disrespect continues. This alone echoes, not just at the Bangalore conference of the RSS, but even in Pappapatti. The tyranny, 'live in the mercy of the majority' extends there. The revolutionary Dr.Ambedkar was very careful in ensuring that such a tyranny of the majority must not enter through the doors of Parliament.

On 6 May 1945, he spoke prophetically regarding this in a public meeting organized by the Scheduled Caste Federation. Even before drafting the Indian Constitution he made precautionary proposals about the rule of the majority. Notably, based on the then existing population, he mentioned along with the necessary statistics how the representative ratio in the Parliament must be.

That is, the 55 percent Hindus must be given a 40 percent representation, the 29 percent Muslims a 32 percent representation, the 14 percent Scheduled Castes a 20 percent representation, 1.6 percent Christians a 3 percent representation and the 1.4 percent Sikhs a 4 percent representation. He stressed that only then would there be politically-based majority and the democratic rights of the minorities would be safeguarded.

The Revolutionary Messiah of Two Hundred Million Dalits

He noted that the formulation must be in such a way that if all the said minorities organize together, they can form the Government without the mercy of the majority. The reduction of the Hindus' 55 percent into 40 percent was only to prevent the tyranny of the majority. He said it was necessary for the remaining (15%) from such a reduction to be distributed among all the minorities, taking into account their respective social, educational and economic backgrounds. He greatly emphasized that the population-based majority must not be established as the political majority, cautioning that such a formation cannot be accepted theoretically or justified in practice. Being dependent on the minority on a political basis would prevent the tyranny of the majority.

Hence he has drafted the Constitution only with such a kind of farsightedness. That is why, to establish the religious majority as a political majority, they are anxious to throw away the existing Constitution and bring in the Uniform Civil Code. Looking at it superficially, the argument that 'the representation of the majority must be in a majority' appears fair.

But that is not democratic! Democracy is based on equality! Anything opposed to equality is anti-democratic! So, it will be revealed that it is opposed to equality! The statement of the RSS stressing the dominance of the majority is evidence that only such a Manu Dharma law rules the Indian land. Further, the ratio of Hindu and Muslim victims in the Gujarat-related violence is 1:12 serves as an evidence of this. In India, the minority is being understood as Muslims. Only on the basis of that idea, it is argued that the Hindus are the majority. The fact that apart from the Muslim minority, several communities such as Christians, Sikhs, Dalits, Tribals, Anglo-Indians are contained in it, is turned down in practice. Thus, the very parliamentary structure, which safeguards the fundamental livelihood rights of all these minorities, will protect democracy.

So protection of minorities must be considered only as a protection of democracy, and it must not be considered as a protection of the Muslim minority community alone. Because of this trend of consideration, horrors like the Gujarat carnage continue! Thus, it is not about whether the majority is for the Hindus or the Muslims! It is for equality and democracy alone!

10 April 2002

w.i.d.e. a.n.g.l.e

POLITICS IN TAMIL NADU
Reeling Around Cinema

Politics in Tamil Nadu has been revolving around the cinema for half a century. It is not possible to imagine Tamil Nadu politics without cinema. Parties use cinema as the foremost and potent tool for political victories.

Cinema has that great talent of winning crowns by driving the people into intoxication and defeating them! That is why, Annadurai invited MGR by calling, 'Just show your face! Thirty lakh votes will be amassed!' From that day till now, cinema is overpowering Tamil Nadu politics! Congress, which ruled Tamil Nadu for over thirty years, was overthrown by cinema! In the circumstances of that day, Annadurai's intellectual prowess and oratorical ability changed the course of Tamil Nadu politics itself ! The Dravidian party came to power! Cinema plays a major role to the extent that from 1967 till today only the Dravidian parties have alternately ruled Tamil Nadu continuously. From the condition of using cinema for politics it has evolved today to the state where 'cinema itself is politics'.

From MGR being made use of by the situation changed, and later, MGR himself became the Chief Minister. It went to the extent that while he was alive it was impossible to defeat him; in fact, he was able to capture power lying in an American hospital. Cinema had bound up the people to that level! What V. R. Nedunchezian, who was the Finance Minister in MGR's cabinet, once spoke at a public meeting revealed the strength of cinema. He said: 'As of today, there are two thousand eight hundred theatres in Tamil Nadu! Of that, even if the movies of new faces or old faces starring anybody runs in eight hundred theatres, in two thousand theatres only *Puratchi Thalaivar* (lit. revolutionary head) MGR's movies are being screened! So till 2010 only the rule of Puratchi Thalaivar will take place in Tamil Nadu!' The kind of intimacy between power and cinema can be understood from his speech.

Karunanidhi who became the Chief Minister after Annadurai was also very closely connected to cinema! If MGR reached the heights of fame by playing the hero in films, Karunanidhi rode the chariot of fame by being the hero of the script. Perhaps because of this, it was Karunanidhi who became the next Chief Minister even though at that time there were any number of political experts who were intimate with Annadurai. Although he had the writing prowess and oratorical skills like Annadurai, it is an undeniable truth that cinema gave him a hand!

In the same manner, like Karunanidhi and MGR, the current Chief Minister Jayalalitha is also a cinema mould! If it was possible for Jayalalitha to become the Chief Minister even though there were several senior leaders to succeed MGR, it is an undeniable truth that only the cinema fame helped her! Hence Tamil Nadu politics is ruled by cinema for the last thirty years and more. Only on that basis, it is now being sensationally talked about everywhere that 'Rajinikanth is the next Chief Minister!' Debates take place arguing whether he would come to politics or he wouldn't. On another side, the news is being spread that actor Vijaykanth is the next Chief Minister. So the plight of Tamil Nadu politics is that only those somehow linked to cinema can become the next Chief Minister!

Till today, cinema was taken as a background for politics! Or cinema celebrities were in the forefront of politics! But today, actor Rajinikanth makes politics as a background for his cinema! 'Now he is coming,' 'Tomorrow he is coming'. In this manner, Rajinikanth's entry into politics, is spoken about, and is made to be spoken about in various hues and shades! 'When is he going to act again?', even that becomes the newspaper headlines! After a gap of three years, when it was announced that he is 'Coming Again', from that day, in all dailies, page after page, photographs and news items about his films kept arriving! Even in an English daily, photographs and news about his film '*Baba*' occupied an entire page. '*Baba*' is yet to become a movie! But there is a great sensation that it has been sold for several crores! A weekly magazine held a contest for readers about what dialogues he would deliver in '*Baba*'! Why is the fact that he is going to act in a film talked about so sensationally? More than the fact that 'he is acting in a film', 'He is plunging into politics' is made into an expectation and they are sensationalizing it.

How can those who impose such sensationalism with the motive of profit and political benefit, think about the degradation of the younger generation? Once, during a Deepavali when a Rajinikanth film was not released, a youth from Madurai draped firecrackers all over his body and set himself afire and burst to death! He dared to commit suicide! Like this how many thousands of youth are aimlessly drifting, mentally ill and their minds confused with the cinema obsession! In this manner, cinema dominates all fields in Tamil Nadu unlike any other state ! Recently there was a people's protest taking place in Karnataka! There was a great agitation that Tamil dialogues must never be allowed in Kannada cinema! Being afraid of the protest of the Kannada people, the producer of the movie promised to remove the Tamil dialogues; only then they gave him the permission for shooting. The people there are overpowering cinema instead of allowing cinema to rule over them! It is revealed from their protest that instead of allowing cinema to be a determining force, they are the determining force! The Tamil people don't have any worries about all that! When they are deep in the cinema stupor, can they think about it? For the people who were once eager, 'Will *Basha* come to rule the country? Or will *Padayappa* come?' the current worry is, 'Will *Baba* come?'* For how many more years will Tamil Nadu politics continue to reel around cinema? One's head is reeling!

24 April 2002

---

* *Basha, Padyappa and Baba* are titles of movies starring actor Rajinikanth

s.h.a.m

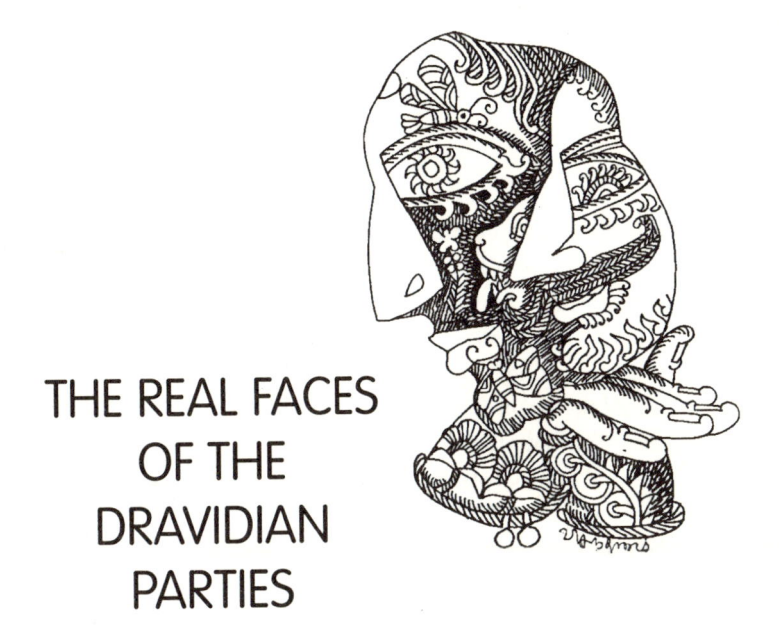

THE REAL FACES OF THE DRAVIDIAN PARTIES

It is eleven years since that horrifying cruelty which seeped the whole world in shock took place. That is, in 1991, while campaigning for the General Elections in Tamil Nadu, all of a sudden, the former Indian Prime Minister Rajiv Gandhi was brutally assassinated.

Eleven years have rolled by since that assassination took place. After such a long interval, in a sudden manner giving rise to sensationalism, a resolution was passed in the Tamil Nadu Legislative Assembly: 'LTTE leader Prabhakaran must be arrested! If it is not possible for the Lankan Government to arrest him, the Indian Government must send its Army and he must be captured!' That resolution which was proposed by the Tamil Nadu Chief Minister was passed, overcoming opposition from a few opposition parties and with the support of a few opposition parties including the Tamil Manila Congress (a breakaway faction of the Congress, that has since merged). After the interval of so many years, why this resolution only now? After the assassination of Rajiv Gandhi, for five years Tamil Nadu was ruled only by the same ADMK! What necessity arose in today's situation which was absent then? No one here has announced that 'there is no connection between Rajiv Gandhi's assassination and Prabhakaran' or that 'he cannot be arrested'.

The Indian Government or the Indian Prime Minister has not announced any single opinion anywhere like that in support of the LTTE. In a situation like this, it is not known what need arose for such a resolution.

When Prabhakaran who was in hiding in the dark and dense forests for a prolonged period of time met reporters all of a sudden, he attracted the attention of international countries towards the Eelam problem. Prabhakaran, who met approximately more than 600 international journalists, said, 'The assassination of Rajiv Gandhi is a sad incident' and he also mentioned, 'it is not possible to tell more opinion about it, since a case relating to it was under inquiry.' In that very long interview which extended for over two hours, he also said, 'In the past and even today, we greatly love peace.'

Through that incident, the entire attention of the world was heaped on Prabhakaran. That resolution was passed in the Tamil Nadu Legislative Assembly only in such a sensational situation.

The Tamil Nadu Chief Minister Jayalalitha is furiously roaring, 'Prabhakaran is guilty of murder! How can he give interviews like a people's leader?' Is Prabhakaran's openly coming to light and giving interviews the reason for her frenzied emotions? The question arises that if by chance he had remained underground instead of giving an interview in that manner, would the Tamil Nadu Chief Minister have maintained silence, saying that there was no necessity to arrest him? The murder case on Prabhakaran is alive! The Central Government has not dismissed the petition. To have passed that resolution in this state of affairs prompts one to think whether the State Government suspects the Central Government? Generally, rather than seeing Prabhakaran as a terrorist or an extremist, the BJP which functions based on the doctrines of Hindutva, views him as an Hindu opposing Buddhism. Whether Prabhakaran realizes himself as a Hindu is a different matter! The BJP has the pro-Hindu religious perspective that Prabhakaran opposes Muslims and Buddhists. It is possible to see, that on the same basis, a few Dalit organizations here view Prabhakaran as a Hindu and Chandrika as a Buddhist; and consider Prabhakaran who opposes Buddhism as an enemy of the Dalits and Chandrika as a sister.

It is shocking when we come to know that there also exists the perspective of viewing the Eelam liberation struggle as a religion-related sectarian issue instead of considering it as an ethnic problem. One feels like thinking that, 'is the BJP which considers Prabhakaran as a Hindu probably involved in the efforts to protect him? On that basis only, is the Tamil Nadu State Government doubting the Central Government?' and so on.

Several people fear that because of this resolution of the Tamil Nadu Government more than Prabhakaran getting arrested, the formation of peaceful situation in Sri Lanka may be affected. It is a little consoling that a fresh situation has arisen where the LTTE leader Prabhakaran has come forward to cooperate with the great efforts of the Norwegian Government and Sri Lankan Prime Minister Ranil Wickremesinghe towards a peace initiative. The Tamil nationalists are silently fretting that when even the Sri Lankan Government, which met heavy losses for over twenty years and was crippled by the economic crisis, has forgotten all that and is now extending its hand towards peace, the Tamil Nadu Government has passed this resolution in a way of spoiling the peace situation. On the day the resolution was passed the PMK, the Viduthalai Chiruthaigal, CPI and CPI(M) walked out of the assembly openly opposing this resolution.

Opposing the resolution doesn't mean that the assassination of Rajiv Gandhi is being justified! Nobody can justify the assassination of Rajiv Gandhi on a humanitarian basis! Anyone connected with that assassination must be arrested and must be punished; nobody can have a different opinion! But considering that the LTTE is being opposed, must an ethnic liberation be endangered? In that manner, because this resolution of the Tamil Nadu Government has been passed during a milieu of reconciliation, it is a hard truth that more than being against the Tigers, it is against the Tamil race, it is against the liberation of the Tamil race itself. The stand of the DMK when such a resolution was passed, brings into question the nationalist feeling of the DMK. More than exposing the DMK's confused state, its 'neutral' stand also makes it possible to infer the ulterior motive of the ADMK Government. That is, if the DMK opposes the Tamil Nadu Government's anti-LTTE resolution, it will be in support of the Tigers! Therefore, a situation may be formed in which the Congress—which severely hates the LTTE—might hate and become an enemy of the DMK.

The crisis for the DMK is whether to oppose the Congress or to oppose the Tigers. If a situation arises where the DMK has to quit the BJP front, it would have to form an alliance with the Congress. In this state of affairs, the DMK is taking a neutral stand to escape from opposing the resolution and seeking the hatred of the Congress or supporting the resolution and bringing into question its Tamil racial sentiments! In a position lacking equal strength, to take the neutral stand will only be in support of the powerful force. So through this resolution of the Tamil Nadu Government, which is against the Tigers, it is known that it is the ADMK's ulterior motive to bring the DMK into such a crucial position.

Thus, the concern of the ADMK Government which passed the resolution opposing the Tigers eleven years after Rajiv Gandhi's assassination took place, and the neutral stand of the DMK which had to escape a political crisis, again and again confirm their 'competitive politics'.

Even if the ADMK and DMK properly show their face to the public saying, 'sympathy over Rajiv Gandhi,' 'affection for the Tamil race,' the reality is that it is not the real face!

08 May 2002

e.x.p.e.r.i.e.n.c.e

LEGISLATIVE ASSEMBLY
Not for the Last

For over the last month, heated debates are taking place in the Tamil Nadu Legislative Assembly in an ear-tickling manner over the Governor's speech and the department-wise demands of budgetary allocation. The activities of the ruling party and the approach of the Assembly head were in such a manner that the opposition parties often walked out.

Specially, DMK, the main opposition party, staged walkouts to the extent that of the days on which the assembly was held, only the number of days when the DMK did not walkout was less! Some days the DMK members were also evicted by the security guards of the assembly. DMK member Parithi Ilamvazhuthi was punished in such a manner that it was not possible for him to even come to the assembly during the last two weeks. A fragrant harmony springs between the ruling party and the opposition party! Rather than speaking about the people's problems, they praised individuals.

Everyone in the ranks of the ruling party, including the ministers, show a lot of interest in singing paeans in praise of the Chief Minister and in ridiculing the former Chief Minister.

Chief Minister Jayalalitha, while responding in the Legislative Assembly to the DMK President Karunanidhi's criticism of her speech delivered at the convocation ceremony of the Dr. Ambedkar Law University, ridiculed him saying that the 'DMK leader Karunanidhi doesn't know English.' She responded in that manner against the DMK leader's criticism relating to news reports that she had mentioned, 'Though the Law University was setup in the DMK regime, the idea for it had been conceptualized in the previous ADMK regime itself.'

After the Chief Minister said that Karunanidhi did not know English, even the members who had not the faintest idea about English, thumped their desks and enthusiastically cheered. Does it mean that all those who do not know English are disgraceful? The question arises if they are to be mocked at.

Will this not implicate the crores of ordinary people who do not have the faintest idea of any other languages other than their mother tongue? Why, will it not also indicate great leaders like Kamaraj and MGR who obtained a permanent place in the people's hearts? So, when the Chief Minister herself is particular about provoking and instigating the DMK members, must the ministers be mentioned? While responding to the grant-of-aid demand for his department, in the beginning itself the Social Welfare Minister spent a great deal of the time only in severely lashing out indirectly and directly against Karunanidhi. The Chief Minister greatly enjoyed it, and did not disapprove of it either by gestures or by telling him to speak relating to his department! Instead she supported it in a manner of further encouraging the Minister's speech. Facing the DMK members who expressed their dissent over his speech, the Chief Minister interfered and said, "Why are you getting angry? Why are you giving the acceptance that only your leader is being talked about?"

The speech made by the Social Welfare Minister, with the intention of deriding Karunanidhi, greatly debased the poor and the lay people.

Indirectly hitting at, and blaming Karunanidhi; and on the other hand, singing the Chief Minister's praise, the Social Welfare minister said, 'Our leader didn't come to Madras in a torn kurta carrying a tin trunk! Our leader is a golden leader who was born with a silver spoon.' Though this hint was aimed at Karunanidhi, doesn't it reveal the opinion that wearing torn clothes and keeping tin trunks are disgraceful? Is there no difference between speaking on party platforms and speaking in the Legislative Assembly? The entire nation knows the types of speeches that have been delivered rebuking each other in the DMK and the ADMK daises during the last thirty years. But is it nice to speak in the Legislative Assembly like speaking in a party public meeting? Can everybody taking birth in this land be born with a silver spoon? If by chance Karunanidhi had come to Chennai in those days with a torn kurta and a tin trunk, it only displays his poverty. Is it human culture to mock that poverty?

Mocking a person's poverty only means mocking the poverty of the crores of lay people living below the poverty line. They toil like bulls in the blazing sun and pouring rain and soaring dust—are the proletariat responsible for their poverty? With no oil to apply on their matted, unkempt hair, without even a set of clothes to change into, wearing tattered clothes that cannot be washed often, unable to make both ends meet, those who wear out their bones to earn the gruel which fills half their stomachs—who is responsible for the poverty of the working class? The exploitative methods—which prevail in this social setup—of stealing the people's labour, are the cause! Will anyone who realizes this, on seeing the victims of cruel poverty, laugh until his mouth hurts? Lacking even a little of such class perspective a few people are daring to mock poverty, instead of worrying about, or rising against it.

In the same manner, lacking the working class perspective, even the Social Welfare Minister maliciously pointed out and derided the predicament of poverty!

Likewise, the Revenue Minister Thalavai Sundaram who provided an explanation for a calling attention motion, remarked that the daily-wage earning slum-dwellers are encroachers. A month ago Ambedkar Nagar, a Dalit ghetto in Chennai's Ashok Nagar,

The ruins of Ambedkar Nagar: A Dalit ghetto in Chennai

was completely burnt to ashes. People are struggling amidst that charred ash with tears and screams! The heart of the Government didn't even melt enough to construct a temporary shed to provide them shelter. In an explanation regarding this, during a calling attention motion, the minister mentioned these people were encroachers. Encroachment is different! Refuge is different! When people come from villages to cities, in search of livelihood, in search of a place to stay, they build their huts in empty unoccupied Government-owned land—the Government must consider it only as a refuge. To consider it as an encroachment only displays the exploitative perspective of the rulers.

A person who constructs a hut so tiny that there is not even enough space inside it to lie down comfortably: is he an encroacher? Even if it is said, 'That place is required by the KK Nagar hospital! So, the slum dwellers must leave it,' it is not wrong. But to portray as encroachers—these patients of poverty who eke out a day-to-day living by working on the roadside as construction labourers and as trash-pickers—is it not crueler than all these cruelties? In this manner, the debates that took place during the beginning of this session, bring into question the democracy of the Legislative Assembly itself.

Permission was not granted to speak condemning the murder of democracy in Pappapatti and Keeripatti where the elected Panchayat presidents were threatened and made to resign! But lots of time is being bountifully given for singing paeans and for abusing! The unnecessary debates and wasteful talk in the beginning of this session have again confirmed that the Legislative Assembly is not the forum for the deprived—the toiling masses—the last people.

22 MAY 2002

p.r.e.s.i.d.e.n.t.i.a.l. e.l.e.c.t.i.o.n

HIS EXCELLENCY: NEEDED AGAIN!

The chief of the three armed forces!

The first citizen among the hundred crore Indian citizens! But, can he implement his power? Can he guide the Government according to the Constitution? Can he at least deliver his speech in the Republic Day and Independence Day celebrations the way he desires? Is he just a powerless decorative doll? Is he the approval-stamp, which the powers that be use in any place they want?

As if in an answer to all these questions, the first and only President who pulverized all the earlier meaningless traditions and left an historical imprint is the Hon. K. R. Narayanan. He crushed all the typical attitudes set by the Indian Presidents till now and created new traditions.

It was customary for the earlier Presidents to generally visit Hindu places of worships like temples and tanks. In earlier times, it was an inevitable duty to take part in the proceedings involving a specific religion such as going to the Tirupathi Devasthanam and doing an *Anga Pradishtinam* (rolling oneself clockwise around the inner passage of a temple in fulfilment of a vow), or getting the blessings of the Kanchi Sankaracharya! Religion and caste-related cultural practices are the democratic rights of an individual! Even if it is uncivil for others to interfere; when the actions of the President come to light instead of being confidential, it creates immense influence in the political field and in the social organization.

The President's participation in functions related to a specific religion becomes great propaganda for the rituals and customs of that religion. Without getting stuck in any such controversy at any point of time, and without having the identity of any one religion, the Hon. K. R. Narayanan effectively guided the Indian republic as its President for a five-year period. He is the first and only President who did his duties with vigour according to the Constitution without whiling away the past five years in visiting temples to seek the blessings of sadhus and sanyasis, performing yagnas, asking for predictions, or vacationing abroad with his family.

Many people are of the view that he became the President only because he is a Dalit! They even say so! Those who have spent a long time in public life will know that his intellectual prowess, hard labour and immeasurable sacrifice alone made him occupy very eminent positions. Before he became the Indian President, he served as an Indian diplomat in several countries. Even during the period he served abroad as a diplomat, instead of whiling away time by considering that post as merely decorative, he functioned constructively with energy and motivation and left an historical mark! Only as a result, fame poured in his direction! He rose as the President of the Indian Republic! Even though he rose to the pinnacle of glory he showed concern for all the grassroot people.

He left an imprint by completely changing the situation where it was traditionally seen as an act of transgression to interfere in governmental policy decisions, for he ensured that even the President could voice his opinions about such policy decisions. Particularly, he is the first and only President who pointed out that reservation was not followed in the Supreme Court and stressed that reservation must be followed even in that type of forum. We can know from this act that he had deep concern in ensuring that social justice should be safeguarded, from top to bottom, in all areas.

Further, in a situation where the Central Government was intensely privatizing all the public sectors, he realized that consequently the social justice called reservation would be snatched away; so, he declared in his speech to the people of the nation that reservation must be implemented even in the private sectors. When the Central Government had not taken any policy decision on the question of implementation of reservation in the private sectors—when it had not even thought about this—in such circumstances, he recorded his view that reservation must be implemented in the private sectors.

Moreover, he mentioned in his speech that ordinary men and women are living defenceless in the current social setup; and referring to the attack on the Parliament, he said that because of the sacrifices of such simple families, the nation and the Government are safe. In his Presidential address on Republic Day, he remembered the security guards who sacrificed their lives during the attacks that took place in the Parliamentary premises and he mentioned that today the nation and the Government are protected because of the great sacrifices of such lay people.

Moreover, he cautioned that extremism and terrorism would increase if legal safeguards were failed to be given to such subaltern Dalits and women. His speeches confirm that the post of the President is not a rubber-stamp to be used by the ruling party whenever necessary. At the same time it also confirms that he has left his impression by being cooperative to the ruling authorities in the manner of safeguarding the Constitution.

Instead of just being a stamp, President K. R. Narayanan left his imprint on history. So if he is again reelected as the President it will be a protection for the nation and the people.

In a milieu where the state of Gujarat has been burning since the last two months, and at a time, where thousands of corpses are burning, it is impossible to imagine the plight of the nation, if a religion-oriented one-sided President is sworn in. In these circumstances, it is a necessity of the times that the Hon. K. R. Narayanan, who is foresighted, respected by both the ruling and opposition party members and filled with humanitarianism and secularism, must again lead the Indian nation. It is the necessity of today. Whether he is close to the ruling party or whether he is close to the opposition party is not significant, it is important that a person full of humanism and secularism becomes the President.

Because the Hon. K. R. Narayanan is completely qualified and has made a mark in that manner, on 17 May 2002, in New Delhi, the Viduthalai Chiruthaigal has placed its request to Sonia Gandhi, President of the Indian National Congress and Leader of the Opposition in the Parliament, to propose K. R. Narayanan to be the President again.

Not because he is a Dalit! He has extensive political experience! He is well versed in the Constitutional minutiae! He is full of humanitarianism! He is a secularist! Instead of having an insolent attitude, he is filled with composure and patience! He is mature in approach! So his services are needed for the nation! Here, whether a secular Government is formed or not, is not a secular President needed? So we need him again!

05 June 2002

v.e.t.o

NO NEED FOR THE ELECTION COMMISSION!

Surrounded by perplexity and anxiety, 'What will happen? When and where will it flare-up?' somehow the by-elections took place without any violence in a noteworthy manner in the three constituencies of Saidapet, Vaniyambadi and Achirupakkam. There is nothing surprising in the manner in which the election was conducted and in the results of the election also, because the by-elections conducted for the Chennai Municipal Corporation prior to these by-elections served as a precursor. If ballot papers were captured, bogus votes were cast, power was misused, and unprecedented violence and transgressions took place even for an ordinary ward member's election itself, then, must one single out a by-election for the position of a Member of the Legislative Assembly? Except that large-scale violence did not take place as expected by everybody; all other types of violations that flouted the election norms took place without any secrecy at all in broad daylight and dazzling lights!

There were lights all through the streets of each and every constituency, and it was as stunning as a carnival! The entire constituency was decorated with flags and festoons in several colors! There was the parade of vehicles! And fireworks in the sky! At every turn, there were plays and merriment! Enjoyment! There is no limit to such shows of pomp by the political parties! 'What? Prescribed election guidelines? Nonsense! Election guidelines are not to be followed, they are only to be flouted'—to that level, there were activities that did not give a damn! All this is not new in the Indian electoral history! All this is customary!

What was different from tradition was that all the opposition parties, including the DMK have, in one voice, raised the war flag against the ruling party, alleging that electoral malpractices have taken place. Even that voice cannot be said as one voice! The DMK and a few other parties have demanded reelection in Saidapet alone, while the PMK has demanded re-elections in all the three districts!

Both the PMK and the DMK protest as a coalition in New Delhi! But in Tamil Nadu, they have separate agitations! Both the parties are members of the National Democratic Alliance (NDA)! The Indian Election Commission is under the control of the NDA Government of which both of them are a part! So is the protest of the DMK and PMK against the Indian Election Commission which is ruled by the NDA of which they are a part? Or is it against the ADMK Government which rules Tamil Nadu? This remains a question mark. For, the Tamil Nadu Government does not have any power in such electoral proceedings! That is, any State Government does not have the power of holding elections to the Legislative Assemblies and Parliament, or monitoring them, or in preventing or punishing electoral malpractices! It is the duty of every State Government to cooperate with the Indian Election Commission! Otherwise, there is no other power! In these circumstances the Election Commission alone must take responsibility for the malpractices that took place in the by-elections held here.

Hence, on that basis, following the agitations by the DMK-PMK, re-poll has been ordered in just 58 polling booths in the Saidapet constituency! Is this the solution to all those malpractices? If it is so, who will arrest those indulging in malpractices? Who will take action against them? Who will prevent such malpractices and violence from occurring? Doesn't the Election Commission have all the power? Will such malpractices and illegalities not take place when re-polls or re-elections are held? Who will prevent the misuse of governmental agencies by those in power (at the Centre or at the states) when by-elections or general elections take place? Does the commission have the power to do so? 'No,' is the single answer to all these questions! That is the answer shown by the history of the past elections!

If the only powers of the Election Commission are the preparation of voters list, distribution of voter identity cards, printing and distribution of ballot papers, safeguarding the ballot boxes, and announcement of results—those in power or those exerting dominance, instead of making election into a mockery what else will they do? In this situation, what must be scrutinized here: Electoral malpractices? Or the uselessness of the Election Commission? But, the DMK and the PMK are not worried about this! Their only outcry is: 'The ruling ADMK has committed irregularities! Is it fair?' In this situation, it is necessary for the DMK and the PMK to turn back and look at the malpractices and violent rampages that took place during the Parliamentary General Elections of September 1999 in the Chidambaram reserved constituency![1]

The nation witnessed passively while violence and malpractices took place in that constituency on a level unprecedented in Tamil Nadu's electoral history. Even after all the human rights organizations exposed the truths of what took place there, the Election Commission did not take notice at all.

Today, in Saidapet, at least the voters got the right to come to the polling booth! But that day in Chidambaram, voters living in cheris were denied even that right! To ensure that the Dalits must not come to the polling booth, twenty-one cheris were set on fire! Hundreds of people were attacked and sustained grievous injuries! A few lost their lives! More than one and a half lakh voters were prevented from casting their votes! After conducting such violent riots, they seized the ballot papers, and with the collusion of the ruling class, they cast bogus votes and made a mockery of democracy!

Today, only the same people loudly protest. Before joining hands with the PMK in opposing the ruling party ADMK, must not the DMK—which supported all the scenes of the PMK—turn and look back a little at what happened then in Chidambaram?... Should the DMK and the PMK not calculate if they have the competence to condemn such electoral malpractices? Can the electoral irregularities here be weeded out if the DMK and PMK opportunistically condemn it? It is not important as to who commits the electoral irregularities here, or who denounces it. However, when those in power and those who exercise dominance are not bothering about the electoral norms, and when the Election Commission passively witnesses this—the question arises whether such an election is required. The Election Commission that does not have even the power to rebuke those who are violating the rules can be dissolved!

19 June 2002

Notes

1. In the Parliamentary General Elections held in the year 1999, Thirumaavalavan contested from the reserved Chidambaram constituency as a candidate of the third front: the Tamil Manila Congress (TMC)-Viduthalai Chiruthaigal combine. The parties in the fray in this constituency were the ruling DMK-combine constisting of BJP, MDMK and PMK—the party of the dominant caste-Hindu Vanniyars. The other row of allies were Congress (I), ADMK, CPI and CPI(M). Thirumaavalavan polled 2,25,768 votes, the second highest number.

    The constituency, dominated by Vanniyars, an oppressor caste that is represented by the Pattali Makkal Katchi (PMK), witnessed barbaric violence against Dalits. The election campaign by the Viduthalai Chiruthaigal stressed Dalit liberation within the framework of the constitutional scheme. The posters, meetings and other canvassing democratically aimed at consolidating Dalits' concerns and in the entire campaign there was no use of provocative language or counter-productive methods. Yet the Viduthalai Chiruthaigal were not even allowed to campaign peacefully. The entire campaign had to be restricted to a mere ten days owing to the threats from the Vanniyars.

On the polling day, 5 September 1999, volunteers of the PMK (and its electoral ally DMK) ran riot and went on a rampage setting fire to more than twenty-one Dalit cheris and thereby prevented over one and a half lakh Dalits from casting their votes. The Cuddalore District Collector declared that five hundred and four houses had been torched in the district. Properties amounting to crores of rupees was damaged, looted, and plundered. The Vanniyars prevented fire engines from entering the cheris which they had set afire. Dalits were prevented from casting their votes in the cheris of Ambalapuram, Uluthur, Kilangadu, Therku Mangudi, Adhandar Kollai, Kandhan Mangalam, S.Arasur, Theertharpalayam, Agaram, Kechikadu, Naduthittu, Ambedkar Colony, Thilagavalli, Mylambur, Vilangipattu, Puduchathiram, Valipattu, Athikulam, Chellankuppam, Kambali Medu, Beemarao Nagar, Vaiyoor and Valaipanthal. Only in a few pockets where the Dalit concentration was higher could some Dalits cast their votes.

The tactics employed for bogus-voting was varied: polling agents were chased away and the Vanniyar polling agents of the DMK-PMK combine indulged in mass bogus voting; all the Dalit votes were cast by the Vanniyars themselves soon after the polling began (in some places the Vanniyars even cast the vote of the Viduthalai Chiruthaigal polling agent); Panchayat and village heads of the Vanniyar community physically presented themselves before the polling booths and prevented entry of Dalits; Vanniyars issued death threats to Dalits who would vote for the Viduthalai Chiruthaigal; the Vanniyar booth agents applied indelible ink on the hands of Dalits who went to cast their votes but snatched the ballot papers from the Dalits and cast the vote in favour of the PMK.

In spite of the written complaints by the Viduthalai Chiruthaigal to the Election Commission, informing it about the possibility of violence in more than 80 villages, the State Government did not take adequate security measures deliberately. Out of 89 villages mentioned in the written complaints, 80 villages were targeted and the right to vote was denied to the Dalits. The appointment of a great number of Election officers from the Vanniyar caste further aggravated this situation.

Of the 1363 polling booths in the Chidambaram Parliamentary Constituency, there were more than 1000 Dalit polling agents and most of them were driven away by force, evidence that could have been verified by examining the slips in the ballot boxes where the polling agents are required to sign. In the majority of the polling stations, the ballot boxes were collected without the signature of the Viduthalai Chiruthaigal polling agents because they had been arrested or assaulted. Most of the Dalit polling agents, were first-timers in the job, and they were threatened with dire consequences and driven out. Those who resisted were severely beaten up and made to run for their lives. When the polling agents who represented the Viduthalai Chiruthaigal-TMC combine were driven out, bogus votes were indiscriminately cast in favor of the PMK candidate. Worse, the police also arrested 40 election workers, including the chief election agent of the Viduthalai Chiruthaigal from their election office on the night of the election day without any reason. In all this rioting by the caste-Hindus, the police joined in, and wreaked havoc by lathi-charging the Dalits and crushing the cheris. For all this violence, they arrested large groups of Dalits from many of these cheris. The police used extremely abusive language against Dalit women and in some instances sexually assaulted them. To add insult to injury, they broke photos of Dr. Ambedkar and tore-up the election posters of Viduthalai Chiruthaigal. The grain storages and college graduation certificates in the cheris were destroyed. In all the areas where violence was reported, the police only arrested the Dalits and kept them under illegal detention. Even weeks after the election, the police didn't release those who had been taken into custody nor did they at least release the names of those arrested. The entire state force was used to unleash this violence.

Although the pre-planned and systematic murderous attack by the Vanniyars took place right in front of the police, the District Collector and the Superintendent of Police issued statements that the poll had been conducted peacefully and that no unlawful incident had been reported up to the end of polling and that violent incidents had taken place only after 5:00 p.m. when polling was closed. The Election Commission turned down the demand of the Viduthalai Chiruthaigal and its allies for a re-poll/re-election in the constituency although it is empowered to order countermanding of elections when there are instances of booth-capture. The matter was also presented before the President. Caste-fanatic Vanniyar hooligans threatened that if a re-election was to be held in the constituency, a 50,000 member strong Vanniyar gang would burn the homes of all the Dalits; and even if the army was called in this would not be stopped.

E. Ponnuswamy, the elected candidate of the PMK, did not get more than 1 percent of Dalit votes. Most of the Dalits—95 percent and more—had cast their votes for the Viduthalai Chiruthaigal, yet Thirumaavalavan was made to lose the election in this reserved constituency. This election made a mockery of the system of reserved electorates, where even if all the Dalits did not vote for a candidate, he could still be elected as the Dalit representative. The incident served as another crude and brutal reminder of why the revolutionary Dr. Ambedkar wanted separate electorates and the double-vote system.

c.o.n.s.p.i.r.a.c.y

the president's election

PARTY COLOURS ON THE BULL'S HORN

Mr. Abdul Kalam, who is going to become India's new President, has announced, 'More than the fact that I am a Muslim, the fact that I am an Indian is more important.' Through this he has confirmed that his patriotism is of greater importance than his religious attachment. His patriotism is laudable! But the question arises, are those with religious affinity devoid of patriotism? If the answer is yes, then are those who say of themselves as 'Hindus,' without the feeling that they are 'Indians'? If it is so, then is there no compatible relationship between religious attachment and patriotism? Or is the Islamic religious attachment alone opposed to patriotism? Does Muslim mean non-Indian?

So Abdul Kalam offers an assurance by himself, 'I will not behave as a Muslim, I will only behave as an Indian.' To whom is he giving this promise? Is it to the head of the Rashtriya Swayamsevak Sangh (RSS), Sudarshan? Only Sudarshan has insisted that the Muslims in India must adopt the culture of the Hindus and they must live as Indians. Therefore Abdul Kalam promises that he shall function according to the wishes of the RSS and the BJP. That is, it can only mean, 'Even if I am a Muslim here, I shall only live as a Hindu!' By way of strengthening this fact, he says: 'Whatever happened, has happened for the good! Whatever happens, happens for the good! Whatever should happen, will happen for the good!'—very carefully, he hurls a quotation not from the Koran, but from the Bhagavad Gita. Perhaps through this he stresses, 'I shall walk not on the path of Allah, but, accepting the preaching of Lord Krishna, walk on the path of Advani!' Is Abdul Kalam selected for the post of President, because he is a Muslim? Is it because he is an Indian? Or is it because he is a scientist? None of this is the basic truth! The real reason is that K. R. Narayanan must not become the President of the Indian republic once again.

While the Congress, the Left parties and a few opposition parties were discussing that K. R. Narayanan himself can become the President of India again; the BJP was attempting to elect P. C. Alexander, the Governor of Maharashtra. Because the Congress and the other opposition parties did not agree to it, the BJP dropped that effort. The widespread idea is that the Congress did not agree to the candidature of P. C. Alexander, taking into account that in the later days, the BJP may, by showing reason that P. C. Alexander is a Christian, prevent Sonia Gandhi from becoming the Prime Minister; therefore, with the intention of outmanoeuvring the conspiracy of the BJP, it did not accept his nomination. That is, if the BJP takes up the propaganda that it is not good for the nation if at the same time both the President and the Prime Minister are from the minority religion (of Christianity), it will turn into a political crisis for Sonia Gandhi! It is understood that the Congress did not accept P. C. Alexander so as to avoid such a situation. Likewise, the BJP did not wish to propose K. R. Narayanan because in the past, he had created many political crises for them! The BJP did not find it suitable to create such crises for themselves by selecting him again.

K. R. Narayanan had created several new traditions against the existing conventions. The speeches he delivered at important and distinguished functions like the Golden Jubilee of Indian

Independence, Golden Jubilee of the Indian Republic, Golden Jubilee of the Election Commission, pulverized several attempts of the BJP. When a commission headed by Justice Venkatachalaiah was appointed to review the Constitution, K. R. Narayanan severely criticized it. He condemned the ruling party saying, 'Problems or deficiencies are not there in the Constitution created by our founding fathers, on the contrary those implementing it are not proper.'

Due to this, the BJP's dream of amending the law to forbid those with foreign citizenship from becoming the Prime Minister of India and thereby prevent Sonia Gandhi from becoming the Prime Minister was annihilated. Likewise, they also attempted to tamper the election procedures and pave the way for indirect elections—where only the members of the local bodies would be elected directly, and the Members of the Legislative Assemblies, the Parliament and even the Prime Minister would be elected only through these representatives. He condemned the Indian governmental authorities saying that it was an anti-democratic step imitating Pakistan. Consequently, the BJP dropped that effort also. He caused a crisis to the ruling class, by making a note on the file that reservation must be implemented in the Supreme Court and in the private sectors also. The BJP avoided K. R. Narayanan just so that such crises did not come again. There is nothing surprising in this! But in the selection of the President, even more than the BJP's decision, only the decision taken by the National Congress, which has a large vote bank and rules more than ten states, is surprising.

In a situation where the BJP had announced Abdul Kalam as its nominee, despite the fact that the Congress was not consulted, the Congress accepted him as their nominee too! It is not due to generosity. On the contrary, it reveals the incapability of that party!

If Abdul Kalam is out of bounds of criticism, the Congress must have supported the decision of the BJP in the beginning itself. Instead of that, without the strength to compel K. R. Narayanan or without the courage to organize all the opposition parties including the Leftist parties and announce a nominee separately, after deferring a decision for several days in the name of discussion, and finally to support the BJP nominee itself exposes the weakness of the Congress. Instead of opposing the BJP's political games, it is seen that the Congress, like the Dravidian parties of Tamil Nadu, is also caught within the saffron trap.

Not only in the election for the President's post, but generally at the national level, the Congress does not have the necessary strength to unite and work with the Dalit and minority organizations and the scattered opposition parties at the state and central levels. That is why, in Uttar Pradesh the Bahujan Samaj Party (BSP) and in Tamil Nadu, several parties including the DMK and the MDMK are moving intimately with the BJP in a manner contradictory to their doctrines. More than the victory of the BJP's diplomacy, this is a defeat for the Congress, which lacks strategy. In Tamil Nadu, if the Tamil Manila Congress and the Congress combine, can they defeat the Dravidian parties? In today's position, it is obvious that the Congress is unable to team up even with the ADMK! Only in this situation the Congress has fallen into the saffron trap! It has decided to support the nominee of the BJP itself. Because of the 'There Is No Alternative' situation, the BJP and the Congress have elected nuclear scientist Adbul Kalam! This is not something that adds fame to the praiseworthy Kalam! The election of Abdul Kalam—more than being used to cover up the BJP's doctrine of hate towards the Muslims and carnage against the Islamic minority in Gujarat—is the final result of the great efforts undertaken by the RSS and the BJP to ensure that K. R. Narayanan does not become the President again!

Like dabbing party colours on the horn of a bull that toils hard in the paddy fields, they have dyed saffron even on the back of the missile technology scientist Abdul Kalam, who was immersed in nuclear research. He also beautifully sings the Bhagavad Gita! Now, is Abdul Kalam, Krishna who recites the Bhagavad Gita and guides the war? Or is he Arjuna who listens to Krishna's preaching and goes to war? In this situation, the position of the Congress is pitiable! In the coming days too, on which side is the Congress? On the side of the Pandavas? Or, on the side of the Kauravas?

03 July 2002

d.i.s.g.r.a.c.e

'THEY' ARE SUPERIOR TO HUMANS

Anyone with humanism can never tolerate this! The disgrace of a man being forced to eat human excrement has taken place in Tamil Nadu. Till now, no one could have heard of such a disgusting-uncivilized act taking place in Tamil Nadu! In the name of caste, the domineering fanatics have thrust several atrocities on the cheri people. Brutal murders, arson, forced ingestion of cow-dung solution, whipping and such other atrocities have taken place without objection. But for the first time, only in Thinniyam, the village itself gathered to witness the atrocity where two Dalit men were branded with red-hot rods and forced to eat human excrement. This might have taken place earlier, but only now has this crudeness been exposed.

This stain on humanity was staged in broad daylight on 21 May 2002 in Thinniyam village, seven kilometres near Lalgudi in the Tiruchi district. We cringe on hearing about it. But, Subramaniam, a retired schoolteacher, did so without any shame and he enjoyed doing it. It is agonizing and a matter of worry that a teacher himself, who is supposed to educate and protect children belonging to all strata has such cruelty, casteist perversity, and an excrement mentality. His wife, Rajalakshmi, is the former Panchayat President. When she was in power, she took two thousand rupees from the gravedigger Karuppiah as bribe towards building him a 'group house' under the Government-housing scheme. But the house was not built as per her promise. Also, Rajalakshmi did not win during the current Panchayat elections. Because of this, Karuppiah who realized that it was not possible for her to build the house asked her to return the money. When Rajalakshmi's husband, Subramaniam, refused to give back the money, Karuppiah appealed to the village elders. But as usual, nobody gave due consideration to it. So, he tom-tommed, 'I will not do the *vettiyan's* [gravedigger's] work for those villagers who do not come forward to get back my money from Rajalakshmi.' Karuppiah raised the voice of rebellion. A vettiyan is a bonded laborer who is at the beck and call, who rushes and bends and supplicates and works for the villagers.

The problem is, a vettiyan—who must be subjugated and oppressed and must exist by drumming the *parai* in caste-Hindu funerals, digging graves, announcing deaths, chopping firewood, removing dead cattle, announcing village-related news, and who, with the towel worn around the hip, must take the given wages by prostrating flat in reverence—had dared to tom-tom against the feudal lord. More than the fact that he tom-tommed, the foremost problem is that a vettiyan has dared to hold his head high! The fundamental reason is that a man who was tom-tomming the news of death is today tom-tomming the proclamation of war against the landlord. The main reason is more than a self-respect problem for the individual Subramaniam; it is a problem of honour for caste. Ramasamy and Murugesan, who accompanied Karuppiah as he tom-tommed, were caught by the casteist mob, and this cruelty was done to them. When both prostrated and cried 'asking

The Thinniyam Victims Ramasamy, Murugesan and Karuppiah

Thirumaavalavan addresses lakhs of people at a meeting in Tiruchi by Viduthalai Chiruthaigal on 12 Aug 2002 to condemn the Thinniyam atrocity

forgiveness for the mistake of accompanying Karuppiah', the casteist fanatics beat them with broomsticks, kicked them, and still their anger did not subside, so they branded them with red-hot rods. When both trembled, unable to bear it, they were mocked. Is this 'human' psychology?

When the casteist frenzy did not subside even after so much torture, they fetched dried faeces in a winnowing pan, and laughed aloud derisively as Ramasamy and Murugesan were forced to feed it to each other! This was seen by the whole village which had gathered there! Did not a single person among them have humanity! Even though this took place in broad daylight, it did not come to light for a week's time. Later that atrocity was exposed because of the efforts of the Viduthalai Chiruthaigal. Some of the involved have been arrested. Tomorrow, they may be released as innocent! But can Ramasamy and Murugesan and their relatives recover from this dishonour? Can this stain ever be washed off? Is this a disgrace that happened only to both of them? Is this not a disgrace to the human race? After hearing about this, how are the great leaders able to maintain silence? When murders take place in the cheris and the huts are burnt, how are these leaders able to remain without

Aerial view of Viduthalai Chiruthaigal's Tiruchi public meeting on Thinniyam

bothering or condemning it? Leaders who go to the villages of Pappapatti, Keeripatti, meet caste-Hindus there and implore to them, 'When you have Maariamma, why do you need Mary Amma? Hindus do not change your religion!'—how is it possible for them not to bother about the murder of democracy? People who can cry for Dalal Azmi who ran away from Kuwait with her lover to India, how are they unable to even utter a least sign of empathy towards the Dalits? Are the streets of the village the outer limits for the humanitarian and democratic feelings of our leaders? Can it not cross that and enter the cheri? Till now, no one has condemned this! For the Dalit people, not even a drop of a tear, but can't they at least spend a drop of ink!

Even animals do not eat their excrement! But man has forced man to do it! More than those with the name 'human', that had the excrement-reasoning to force another to eat faeces; and more than those that saw it with their eyes and heard it with their ears, and still remained dumb; the animals who do not eat their own excrement and do not force others to eat it are superior!

17 July 2002

l.i.b.e.r.a.t.i.o.n

EELAM IS THE FOETUS OF THE TIGERS

What has happened in Tamil Nadu to the extent that the Prevention of Terrorism Act 'POTA' had to be implemented here? Has national integration and the nation's sovereignty been thwarted? Did anyone here give refuge to the LTTE, which was banned following the brutal assassination of the young Prime Minister Rajiv Gandhi? Did they make arrangements for the boarding and lodging of LTTE cadres? Did they collect and distribute money and property? Did they supply them with weapons? Did they distribute publications supporting the political ideologies of the Tigers? Whatever happened in Tamil Nadu in support of the Liberation Tigers? Suddenly, what need arose here to the extent of using POTA? The ruling authorities mentioned that this law was brought only against those infiltrating into Kashmir from Pakistan and indulging in terrorist activities; and those extending support to such terrorist activities.

All the opposition parties fiercely opposed this law, stating that this law was dangerous and unnecessary and that it would be used to wreak vengeance on political enemies. Even the masses opposed it, fearing that this law could be used against them, particularly against the Muslims and the Dalits. On the national level, great opposition arose! It created turmoil in the Parliament!

Transgressing all this opposition, a joint sitting of the Lok Sabha and the Rajya Sabha was called for, and the 'POTA' was passed. To call for a joint sitting of both the houses is something that happens very rarely. By following such a rare course of conduct the ruling party passed this law very obstinately. It is not known if this law which was brought about in such a manner, is implemented today even in Kashmir. The sudden unleashing of this law in Tamil Nadu has created shock in every sphere.

The arrest of Vaiko, MP, and General Secretary, MDMK and his party men, who are part of the ruling NDA, is very surprising! 'Is this the plight for even those who are in power, even for those who supported the POTA?'—this has created panic among the people. Were they arrested because they supported the Tigers? Or, are they in this plight for having supported the POTA? Therefore, what is known? Are only Vaiko and his party men supporting the liberation of Eelam and the Tigers? The entire Tamil race is morally supporting that Tamil Eelam must blossom! Moral support is only an ideological support! To consider such support as a crime and to engage in arresting Vaiko is a repressive measure of snatching away the right of opinion. Vaiko and his party men are only ideological supporters of the Liberation Tigers, nothing more.

This law has been unleashed for Vaiko having spoken in support of the Tigers in a meeting addressed in some corner in Thirumangalam in the Madurai district. By speaking in support of an organization that has been banned by the Indian Government, is that organization going to grow here? In what way will the LTTE be strengthened if the organizations and leaders in Tamil Nadu support the LTTE? May be, fame might increase for the supporters! What benefit will the Tigers reap due to it? Those who are here, are they going to enrol the youth of Tamil Nadu in the army of the Liberation Tigers? Are they going to extravagantly present guns, missiles, cannons and other weaponry? Of what use will plain talk be? If even this mere talk is not admissible, it is only a fascist repression of the freedom of expression!

How will it become democracy if all the citizens must do just what the rulers think? Even though it is the duty of a citizen to respect the law, how is it right to expect a citizen to behave according to all the wishes of those who enact and implement the law? The only objective is to ensure that an alternative opinion and criticism must not be said against the rulers.

Has public order and peace in Tamil Nadu been disrupted to the extent of utilizing such a repressive measure? Even in the tremulous situation of the assassination of former Prime Minister Rajiv Gandhi, the supporters of the Tigers did express their mere verbal support! At that time too there was the same ADMK Government! There was the same Chief Minister! But such frenzied and severe measures were not taken then. Resolutions against the Tigers were not passed in the Legislative Assembly then! Why such frantic activities only now? It is possible to understand that these measures are taken to sow confusion in the NDA and thereby consolidate the ADMK's presence at the national level! As of today, the ADMK is not there in any alliance on the national level! Moreover, now itself the political parties have started making the moves for the forthcoming Parliamentary elections which will be held in two more years! In these circumstances, it is possible to predict that the ADMK has also started its game. If contradictions arise and clashes explode in the NDA because of these activities of the ADMK Government, the position of the DMK might also end in a crisis! If that happens then not only for the Congress, but for the BJP also, the gates of the ADMK may be opened! Therefore it is possible to visualize the arrest of Vaiko as an action based on political calculations! Although the news being propagated is that Vaiko was arrested because of supporting the Tigers, everybody has realized that it is not the only reason by itself. Vaiko supported the LTTE even at the time he was in an intimate alliance with the ADMK. Even when he was in the DMK, while the DMK supported Sri Sabharatnam, leader of the Tamil Eelam Liberation Organization (TELO), he only supported the Tigers. He continuously supported the Tigers from that time, and today, it is revealed that political reasons are the basis for the law to have leapt on him suddenly.

Leaving this aside, there is not going to be any loss for the Tigers, because of these measures that are being undertaken by showing them as the cause! Possibly, the ADMK may reap political benefit! At the same time, it is a cause for agony that through their opposition to the Tigers, they instigate and develop the 'No to Tamil Eelam' feeling of hatred among the Tamilians in Tamil Nadu. They give the explanation, 'We are not against Tamil Eelam, we are against the Tigers only!' Because Tamil Eelam and Liberation Tigers cannot be viewed in separation from the other, in today's context even the Sinhalese Government that has suffered uncountable loss for more than the last twenty years is coming closer to hold talks with the Tigers. It is not possible to talk of Eelam by avoiding talk about the Tigers! Only the Tigers can give birth to Eelam. Eelam is the foetus of the Tigers. Can it pour without clouds? Can Eelam be obtained without the Tigers? In this context, the question in front of us is whether the Tamil Nadu Government which is fiercely opposed to the Tigers supports Eelam.

With that, the Tamil Nadu Government must also make it clear if the people of Tamil Nadu should support Eelam or not? Following the arrest of Vaiko by the Tamil Nadu Government, a few parties in the NDA have declared that they are going to try to bring in changes in the POTA law. No matter how many changes are brought about, political rivals, the Muslim minority and Dalits will be greatly affected by this law. Therefore, in these circumstances will parties including the DMK and the MDMK raise their voice to abolish this law! Or for the sake of position, will they extend their hands to strangulate the throat of democracy?

31 July 2002

p.l.i.g.h.t

SOMALIA IN TAMIL NADU?

The life of over ten lakh weavers in Tamil Nadu has fallen into the 'starchy' gruel tanks. The life of those who worked hard to clothe others is now in tatters. This is a great shame to the Tamil land!

In the Virudhunagar district, Thiruvilliputtur and many surrounding areas, because of the cruelty of poverty, here and there, the sympathetic are making gruel and serving it to the drought-hit weavers to wet their stomachs. In that manner, for just getting that paltry gruel itself, people are painfully waiting in queues!

Who is responsible for this state of the weavers? What is the reason? What did the Tamil Nadu Government do while the situation of the weavers worsened to the level that they are now standing with their hands outstretched for gruel. Before the public sympathized and started giving gruel to these workers, did the information not reach the Government? Till those in the ranks of the opposition parties declared that they would also open gruel tanks, why did the Government ignore this?

Before the masses rally on the streets, raising flags and thundering demands it will be an ideal of a republic to instinctively know and fulfil the needs of the citizens. Till lakhs of weavers were left on the streets was it not possible for the Government of Tamil Nadu to grasp their plight?

After the passage of so much time, what is the use of the Government offering them free foodstuff? For how long will the Government keep supplying them with free foodstuff? Without resurrecting the crushed weaving industry, how are the shattered lives of the weavers going to be resurrected? The threads required for weaving are not available! For, nowhere is the necessary production taking place either properly or entirely! The cotton mills in Tamil Nadu are being closed down one by one. The reason attributed is that each factory is running at the loss of crores of rupees. Setting aside the factors like who and what is responsible for such loss, the fact is that only the innocent labourers are affected.

With the exception of one or two mills, all the eighteen cotton mills owned by the Government of Tamil Nadu have been closed down. The foremost reason for this is the new economic policies of the State and Central Governments! Not only the cotton mills in Tamil Nadu, but at the national level too, very large mining industries are being shut down or they are being ceremoniously handed over to the private concerns; and the reason concocted is that they are declining industries running on loss. For example, the Kolar gold mines in Karnataka has been downsized from 24000 labourers into 4000 labourers; preparations are underway to shut it down or to sell it to private owners.

The Salem Steel Plant is also suffering the same plight. The new economic policies of the Government, impure administration of the ruling authorities and a complacent approach lacking foresight are the basis for this predicament of the factories. In that manner, the plight of the labourers who had worked in the closed cotton mills, and their families are not known. Apart from this, when even these people do not have work how can the weavers have work? Where is the strength in the weavers to purchase thread from private producers? When the governmental produce stopped, the weavers stopped getting fair price thread!

Further, when the Tamil Nadu Government suddenly dropped the scheme of distributing free dhotis and sarees to more than one crore labourers living below the poverty line that was in practice for so many years, the employment opportunity for the weavers was snatched away. The situation, 'No threads for weaving, no gruel for the stomach' is being produced! It is being talked about that the foremost reason for the plight of the weavers was the Government's dropping the free dhoti-sari scheme.

After declaring that the free dhoti-saris will be distributed only after a proper list of those below the poverty line was prepared, the scheme was completely dropped by the Government. Because of that, those who dipped new clothes into starch that day are now aching to wet their stomachs with starch.

If such a horrid poverty has affected the weavers in the southern districts, on another side, in the districts like Tanjore, Nagapattinam, Thiruvarur, Pudukottai, Tiruchi, Cuddalore, farmers and farm labourers are in the same predicament. In those districts, the poor people are migrating from the villages to cities like Mumbai, Bangalore, Chandigarh, and Chennai. Moreover, without employment opportunities the plantation workers in the Nilgiri tea estates are also suffering from hunger and starvation for the past six months and more. Hired farm labourers, tea plantation workers, weavers—it has not fully come to light that a great section of the proletariat are becoming victims of starvation in this manner.

Opening 'gruel-tanks' for the weavers has taken place in Rajagopalachari's period (1950s) itself. The same situation is continuing today! The plight of the weavers is exposed because of the relief measures like the gruel tanks. But the plight of the daily wage earners, hired labourers, plantation workers and other scattered workers is being charred in the dark. It will continue till the proletariat realize that all this is the outcome of the terrifying economic policy!

Only because the Tamil Nadu Government is determined to implement the policy of globalization through privatization and liberalization, it is not worrying about the gruel-tanks, not displaying concern about the implementation of the free dhoti-sari scheme, and it is announcing that it shall sell the dhotis and saris in the ration shops. Those who have accepted the policy of globalization can never worry about the proletariat! On one side flourishing richness! On the other side, horrifying and harsh poverty! This is the contradicting evolution of privatization—liberalization—globalization! If such conflicting growth and the Tamil Nadu Government's complacency that doesn't care about the subaltern proletariat continues, in the category of weavers, hired farm labourers, tea plantation workers, the list of proletariat will lengthen! Here, a 'starvation state' will be formed. According to the wishes of the caste leaders whether caste based separate states are formed or not, the formation of a 'Somalia' cannot be stopped!

14 August 2002

h.o.p.e

A RAW TAMILIAN IS NEEDED!

From now onwards, it has become a questionable matter if a Tamilian in Tamil Nadu can discuss about the Tamil language or the Tamil race. To that extent, the feelings of the Tamilians towards their language and race has been cruelly suppressed in Tamil Nadu. Such types of anti-Tamil repressive measures have been unleashed both directly and indirectly. The ruling class is determined to entirely destroy and annihilate Tamil national consciousness by not only using a severe law like 'POTA' but also by letting loose all types of repressive laws that exist. For instance, the Tamil Nadu Government evoked the criminal *'Guerilla'* Act of 1908 (Amendment Act) and banned the

Tamil Desiya Iyakkam (Tamil Nationalist movement). Not being satisfied even with the imprisonment of the movement's President Pazha Nedumaran and the General Secretary Suba Veerapandian under POTA, the Tamil Nadu Government's act of banning the Tamil Nationalist movement, which was ethically functioning under their leadership, brings to light the anti-Tamil behaviour that has been extensive and deep-rooted in the minds of the ruling powers.

What has the Tamil Nationalist movement done for it to be banned? Apart from the fact that persons belonging to the organization righteously support the Liberation Tigers on an ideological level, is there evidence anywhere that they have participated in violent or anti-people terrorist activities? When the leaders of the Tamil Nationalist movement expressed their opinion in support of the LTTE which was banned under POTA, they were imprisoned under the selfsame POTA; even after this, it is not known what political crisis arose in Tamil Nadu that the mass movement itself had to be banned!

Is it only with the support of the Tamil Nationalist movement that the Liberation Tigers have been clashing with the Sinhalese Army for so many years? Are the Liberation Tigers unable to function today because this movement has been banned? In what way can the Tamil Nationalist movement or the Tamilians in Tamil Nadu help the immensely capable Liberation Tigers who have withstood a quarter century of conflict with the military units of a country? Are the Liberation Tigers in such a position that they seek the sympathy of the Tamilians in Tamil Nadu for their defence?

When the position is that those in Tamil Nadu cannot help the Liberation Tigers in any manner, is it not solely a blatant anti-Tamil measure to let loose POTA on the Tamilians and ban the Tamil Nationalist movement by blaming the Liberation Tigers? What does it show when parties like the DMK, and the PMK maintain silence while this sort of planned unleashing of repressive measures is taking place in the political arena? It only exposes that more than the ruling parties, which unleash POTA against the Tamil race, parties like the DMK, MDMK, PMK, which openly support

POTA, being silent in such critical situations, are greatly betraying the Tamil race. Today, the parties that sought political benefit by talking about the Tamil language and the Tamil people are on one side using repressive measures against the Tamil race, and on another side they are betraying the Tamil race, which is unforgivable in history!

While such an anti-Tamil betrayal and extermination is being staged in the political arena, very ruinous and degrading work is going on in the cultural sphere also. Particularly over the last thirty years and more, Tamil youth are being castrated through the field of cinema.

Without any feeling for race or language, the younger generation is deteriorating; caught in the illusion of cinema they build temples for actresses and offer oblations of milk for cutouts of actors. Instead of respecting the elders who have struggled for the welfare of the nation and race, they are wandering in search of their leaders in the theatres itself; they are even searching for the Chief Ministers of tomorrow! Those in the cinema world continue to capitalize on this fan-following among the youth and mercilessly exploit them.

No object comes to the market without being produced! But actor Rajinikanth's films are sold for several crores even before they are produced. These are only acts that exploit the fan-feeling among the Tamil youth! An illusion, 'Now, he is going to enter politics' has been created since the past fifteen years and through that the youth are being exploited in the most horrible manner.

Moreover, propaganda in support of religion takes place in his movies. Further, opinions are being thrust to vulgarize Periyar who preached the rationalist ideology. All this cannot be considered as a premeditated action of an individual called Rajinikanth. This can only be a conspiracy of a gang whose intentions are against the Tamil race! Not only the Rajinikanth film *Baba*; one can see that the Tamil cinema world itself is not bothered about the welfare of the people of Tamil Nadu! Tamil cinema is trapped in the dominance of a gang which lacks the attachment for the language, to the extent that movies which are shot in Tamil language are given English names like *Youth, King, Red, Junction, One Way …*

On one hand, this gang fleeces and exploits the resources of Tamil Nadu; and on the other hand, they are castrating Tamilian youngsters to the extent of leaving them deprived of any feelings for language or race. That is why, a fan who wanted his wife to deliver when the film *Baba* was released, had urged the doctors to perform a caesarean section on his wife to bring forth the baby. That is, he wanted the entry of his child into this world to be a simultaneous occurrence with *Baba* hitting the theatres. To this level Tamilian youth are obsessed with cinema.

In this manner, on one side decline is taking place in the cultural field! On the other side, in the political platform as if to root out the Tamil race, POTA is being let loose to enact repressive measures! Today, forces opposed to Tamil Nationalist sentiments dominate both politics and cinema (which determines politics itself) in Tamil Nadu. As a consequence, we have POTA that oppresses the Tamilians and *Baba* that lures them! If the Tamil language and Tamil race are to be retrieved from such illusion and repression, a raw Tamilian is needed here!

04 SEPTEMBER 2002

c.o.n.t.r.o.v.e.r.s.y

MUSHARRAF IS ALSO AN INDIAN!

'A white woman belonging to Italy thinks of ruling India? That will never take place! It is not permissible! I will campaign all over India against Antonio Maino Gandhi!'—Jayalalitha, the Chief Minister of Tamil Nadu furiously lashed out against Sonia Gandhi, the President of Indian National Congress and Member of Parliament in a press conference on 2 September 2002 where she addressed reporters for over two hours. This has created a great sensation in the political circle. As usual, confusion remains within the Congress party. Because, as far as Tamil Nadu is concerned, for the past thirty-five years, the Congress has been functioning as fronts of the Dravidian parties—as 'ADMK Congress' and 'DMK

Congress.' It has been passing time in Tamil Nadu politics only with the help of one Dravidian party or another. Similarly, seeking the favour of the Congress party at the Centre, the DMK and ADMK used to compete with each other and kept renewing their ties with the Congress. In the present situation, there is a stiff competition between DMK and ADMK to obtain the favour of the BJP Government at New Delhi. The ADMK is taking great efforts to remove the DMK, which is part of the NDA, and thereby obtain that position. The DMK is undergoing untold strife in order to retain its place. For this reason it is supporting a cruel anti-people law like the POTA!

Moreover, during the last general elections held for the Legislative Assembly, the DMK gave importance to the BJP at the state level for the sake of seeking the favour of the BJP at the Centre. Even when it was known definitely that the Communist parties, the Tamil Manila Congress, the Congress and such other parties would not enter into an alliance where the BJP was, the DMK placed the BJP, which was in no way stronger than these parties, in the second place in its alliance. That is, even if they were not able to capture power in Tamil Nadu, the DMK was firm in not losing the relationship with the BJP at the Centre. To that extent, even today the DMK is particular in retaining its relationship with the BJP.

Similarly, even the ADMK is making several strategic moves to weaken the DMK at the Centre. At a point of time the DMK and the ADMK used to compete with each other to have ties with the Congress, now that has changed. Today, both the parties are competing to form an alliance with the BJP. As a result, the position of the Congress in Tamil Nadu is unstable. The Tamil Nadu Congress is suffocating, unable to either believe the DMK and thereby oppose the ADMK or vice versa. That is why even after Jayalalitha breathed fire against Sonia Gandhi, calling her 'white woman, swindler and criminal' the Tamil Nadu Congress does not seem to have boiled with anger.

On the contrary, in order not to offend Jayalalitha they are saying, 'This is unnecessary, she is trying to divert the people.'

They are attacking Jayalalitha with arrows made of peacock feathers! Not only nowadays, but for a long time, the DMK and the ADMK have been criticizing the Congress and its leadership. In those days, the DMK vehemently criticized the Congress and its leadership saying, 'The cut-throat culture is Congress culture' and 'Indira Gandhi is a bloodthirsty vampire'. Still, during the time of elections, it is customary for both the DMK and the Congress to forget it. In the same manner only, the ADMK is also handling its relationship with the Congress.

When Sonia Gandhi assumed the post of President of the Indian National Congress, Jayalalitha criticized her as a 'foreigner'! But, afterwards, having forgotten all that, the Congress and the ADMK joined intimately in the Parliamentary General Elections in 1999. In a tea party in New Delhi, Sonia and Jayalalitha, enjoyed each other's friendly company. Subsequently, the ADMK campaigned in the streets of Tamil Nadu with a bid to make Sonia the Prime Minister.

But today, once again, Jayalalitha has raised a battle cry against Sonia! It has to be analysed on what basis has this cry been raised. Is Jayalalitha sloganeering on the basis that 'The sons-of-the-soil must rule the land?' If it is so, is this principle of sons-of-the-soil only for Delhi? Or will it be applicable for each and every state in India? If India is to be ruled only by an Indian, then only a Tamil should rule Tamil Nadu! If India is to be ruled only by an Indian, it is natural for the question 'Who is Indian?' to arise! If a person is Indian by being born in India, then all Pakistanis are Indians! The President of Pakistan Musharraf is an Indian!

Before Pakistan was declared a separate country it only remained within the Indian territory. In these last fifty years how did they become foreigners? While we accept as Indians those who were born here but are abroad, why do we consider those who lived within the same territory and under the control of the same Government, as enemies and foreigners when they established a separate Government for themselves?

If they themselves are not Indians, it is natural for the question to arise whether Aryans are Indians?

Indian history chronicles that thousands of years ago, from regions of Central Asia, the Aryans came into the Indian territory through the Khyber and Bolan Passes!

No historian has opposed this fact till now. Those who wish to oppose it and those who wish to rewrite history have till today not proven the truth of their claims! In this position, will not the question rise if the 'Aryans are sons-of-the-soil' of the Indian nation! If it is said that the Brahmins who are called Aryans, are 'sons-of-the-soil' and are Indians because they have settled here for a long time; then, is it wrong to say that the Pakistanis who have recently separated from us are also Indians? What is the definition of Indians? Is it territory? Or birth? Or class? Or race? If the Aryans who live in India are Indians it also applies for Sonia who lives in India! If the Aryans can rule India, even Sonia can rule it! Is it not a definite truth that Sonia is not of the Dravidian or Tamil race?

25 SEPTEMBER 2002

p.r.i.v.a.t.i.z.a.t.i.o.n

EVEN A PRIVATE GOVERNMENT CAN BE FORMED!

A very large financial establishment with more than two crore shareholders, the 'Unit Trust of India' (UTI) is a public sector undertaking. It was started in 1963 with a capital of five crores; and in the last forty years has expanded and attained a capital valued at around seventy thousand crores. It is a great source of help and unflinching support to the functioning of the Central Government. Till now, it has invested its funds in more than fifty industrial sectors and other establishments. In every establishment, a minimum of 10 to 15 percent of the shares is under its direct control. What has happened now to this successful financial organization that had collected so many investors and raised a great amount of funds within such a short span of time? What else? The UTI organization is going to become a mouthful to the horrid hunger of the policy of globalization that is anxious to swallow the world. All preparations are underway to privatize a public sector concern like the UTI. Like the Salem Steel Plant, which is to be offered to Jindal, the Central Government is preparing to handover the UTI to the Reliance Group.

The Expert Committee and the Federation of Ministers concerned has released this information! We come to know that instead of even selling the UTI organization to the Reliance Corporation, an agreement is going to be made for a complete handover. Those who work in that organization share the opinion that the political parties do not have any concern regarding this. Privatization is not a problem that has happened to the UTI alone! It is a very large threat aimed at all the governmental and public sector enterprises throughout the nation! It is being said that privatization is taking place in order to manage the financial situation and to bring in regularity and propriety in the administration of governmental and public sector enterprises. Further, it is also being said that privatization is essential to cut down on unnecessary expenditure and to increase the savings; and through this provide excellent maintenance.

But in reality such liberalization, privatization, etc., are being imposed in order to successfully implement globalization. The capitalist can invest and start his industry in any corner of the world! There will be no barriers! Only then globalization can be successfully implemented! How much liberalization is offered for a new industry to be started, in the same manner, privatization of the preexisting Government industries and public sectors, is another dimension of globalization. Because Government and public sectors employ a large number of workers and employees, liberal expenditure and maintenance are inevitable. Because of this, profit is not up to the expectations. It is the aim of the public sectors to offer employment opportunities to the public and to serve the people! But its exact opposite is the basis for globalization!

Hence, the aim of this policy is to gain profit and to serve the superpowers. Based on this, the General Agreement on Tariffs and

Trade (GATT) agreement has compelled factories lacking profit and public sectors to be shown as declining organizations and offered to private owners. The World Trade Organization (WTO) is showing the way! If the declining industries are to be entrusted to private bodies, the World Bank and the International Monetary Fund are ready to give money liberally for the restructuring.

So, privatization is one procedure for globalization! How can the Indian Government—which defines the Indian economic policy by approving globalization—take interest in the welfare of the Indian people? How can they understand the feelings of the labourers? How will the Central Government—which is involved in rapidly downsizing factories and public sectors, providing voluntary retirement schemes, stopping new employment intake and taking such other measures—abandon privatization? Several sectors under the control of the Central Government are being converted into private sectors. Specially, it is a long time since the education sector came under the dominance of the private players. The technological institutions are transformed into business enterprises; and they are involved in large-scale swindling. Thus, profit is the foremost motive in privatization.

Further, privatization is not only based on the profit motive; it is a cruel poison that kills social justice. Only because of the social justice policy of reservation, it was possible for those who had been cruelly cheated and denied of opportunities for many thousand years to enter into governmental institutions and public sector undertakings. On that basis only, Dalits, backward classes and the most backward classes could step inside a financial organization like the UTI. Now, even that has been privatized. Those opposed to social justice are welcoming privatization with showers of flowers instead of directly saying that reservation is denied through privatization. In this manner, we can realize that privatization is a great enemy of social justice!

In the public sectors, 51 percent of the shares will be in the name of the President of India, they will be the shares of the Government! Because private parties own the remaining shares, even in public sectors there is dominance and interference by these private shareholders. That gang does not hesitate to interfere and obstruct the implementation of reservation in public sectors! Even then, overcoming all this, the Dalits and other backward classes are able to get at least the opportunity to work as the last grade employees in these sectors. The worst effect of privatization is that even such an opportunity will be snatched away.

Moreover, if organizations like the UTI are privatized, several welfare schemes of the Central Government enforced through these organizations may be affected! Especially, the welfare schemes for the children and the aged, implemented on a national level through the UTI may be dropped! Also to prevent the sudden slides in stock market and to break the stagnation in the industrial sectors, establishments like the UTI, Life Insurance Corporation (LIC) and the State Bank of India are great pillars of support! The stability of the financial structure remains a question mark if all these organizations are privatized.

Will privatization be the solution to the decline and fall of the public sector? Who is responsible for this decline? For this too, must the subaltern and backward people be sacrificed? To whom are they going to handover the profit which is gained through privatizing all the public sectors, contemptuously disregarding social justice, downsizing the workplace, using advanced technologies and administrative skills? Is the duty of a Government to serve the people; or, is it to serve the imperialists?

Privatization is a way to globalization! Globalization is the service for the imperialist superpowers! In these circumstances, who is going to be served by the Indian Government's privatization of the public sector establishments like UTI, Salem Steel Plant, etc.? The Indian people? Or, the imperialist superpowers? When the public sector is being entrusted to private corporations, even the Government can be entrusted! Like private sectors, even a private Government can be created! That is just the monarchy of those days!

09 OCTOBER 2002

c.o.n.v.e.r.s.i.o.n

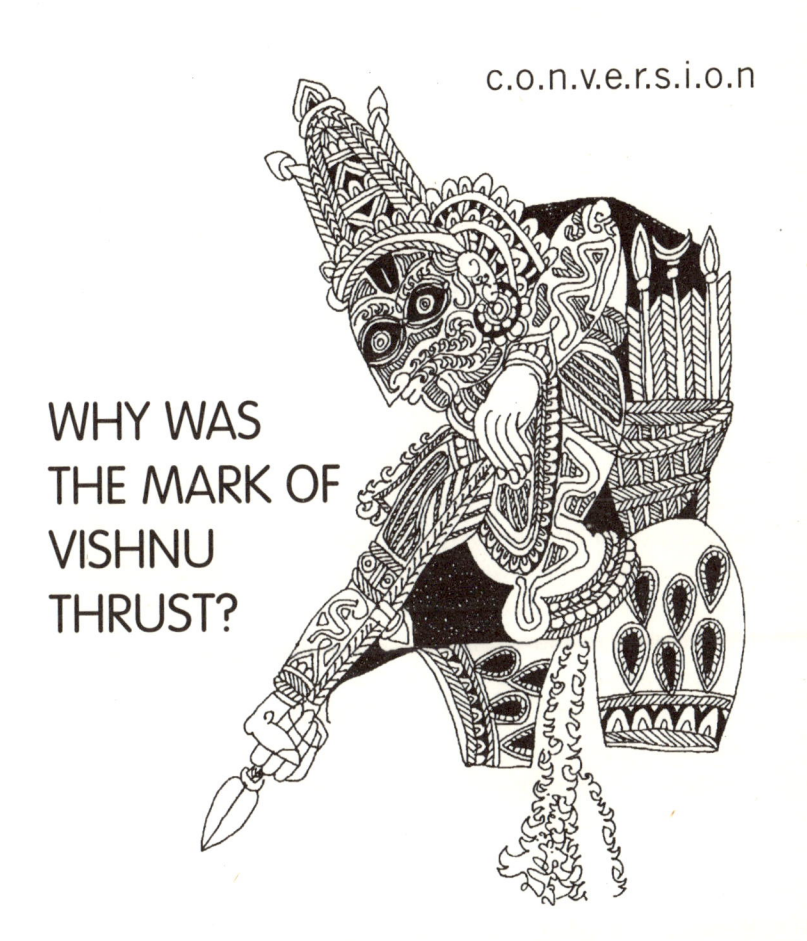

WHY WAS THE MARK OF VISHNU THRUST?

Do you know who was the person who vowed, 'Though I am born as a Hindu, I will not die as a Hindu', and as per that, on the verge of death embraced Buddhism and attained *parinirvan*? He is only the revolutionary Dr. Ambedkar! It was only the revolutionary Dr. Ambedkar who revealed to the world the cruelty of the Hindu religion that oppressed and enslaved the sons-of-the-soil, the original inhabitants of the land, that is, the cheri people who were made into refugees, who lost all their fundamental rights and were deprived of education, land, weapons and power. It was Dr. Ambedkar who provided the unshakable evidence that all of them became victims of this disgraceful position only because they were Buddhists and they didn't accept the *chaturvarna* casteist structure and they did not share any rapport with Hinduism at any point of time. Only to further strengthen that truth and to make firm the anti-Hindutva opposition, Dr. Ambedkar was himself a pioneer who guided the cheri people to embrace Buddhism.

Why did Dr. Ambedkar, who said that Dalits are not Hindus, change his religion? What was the necessity for the change? How is it possible for a person who was not a Hindu, to say, 'I will not die as a Hindu!' A question may arise if it is contradictory! The reason for this is the definition of 'Hindu!' Only this amusing definition categorizes even those fiercely opposing Hinduism as Hindu! Only in that manner, the cheri people—who have absolutely lost their Buddhist identity because of the cruel, unsympathetic repressive measures and have opposed Hindutva for generations and generations—are called Hindus. If a person says that he is not a Hindu, then to prove that he belongs to some other religion, the revolutionary Dr. Ambedkar announced his decision to change his religion and embraced Buddhism. The Hindus are not considering it as an opposition on the argument that as per the Constitution, Buddhism is also a branch of Hinduism, and that embracing Buddhism would not come under religious conversion. To that extent, Buddhism has been annihilated and destroyed that even its footprints don't exist. Still, to renew and establish that Buddhism itself was the earlier lifestyle of today's Dalits; the revolutionary Dr. Ambedkar had adopted such measures.

Dr. Ambedkar adopted religious conversion as a method to oppose and annihilate the inhuman doctrine of life of Hinduism. The poor, ordinary and toiling people who have aligned towards Christianity and Islam in opposition to Hindutva have used the same method for ages and ages. Christianity and Islam have taken root and grown here by presenting such resistance and opposition against Hinduism. That is why, the Hindus are very anxious to uproot Islam and Christianity, the way Buddhism and Jainism were annihilated in those days. The Tamil Nadu Chief Minister has introduced the Prohibition of Religious Conversion Ordinance as an emergency act as an effort to defend herself from the crisis that surrounds her.

It presents a great shock that a Dravidian Party, the ADMK—has sought the favor of those Hindutva upholders in power in Delhi and has tried to show 'this is a Hindutva rule only'—has come forward to do what the BJP itself did not dare do.

Lacking even a needlepoint of determination to prevent or to punish the disgusting activities of the casteist fanatics who disgracefully forced a man to eat faeces in Thinniyam and forced another to drink urine in Goundanpatti, the Tamil Nadu Government has, in such a milieu, not thought of showing the way to protect the self-respect of these victims of torture and humiliation. Instead, it has unleashed the severe devastating law of Prohibition of Religious Conversion Act with the objective of snatching the democratic right of religious conversion.

This law is against the Constitution! Every individual's fundamental right will be snatched away forcefully! What has happened here to the extent that such a cruel law has to be implemented in Tamil Nadu today? Who have announced their decision to undergo religious conversion? Recently, a few college students in Madurai, changed their religion. And news has been released that a few caste-Hindus in the Pappapatti village in the Madurai district have announced their decision to convert their religion and that the cheri people of the Koothirambakkam village in the Kanchipuram district—who were not allowed the enter the temple by the casteist fanatics—have planned to convert to Islam. Because of this, while the guardians of Hinduism were in a state of panic, this ordinance of the Tamil Nadu Government was promulgated by the Governor when the Legislative Assembly was not in session.

It is possible to understand for what, why and for whom this law has been brought about by observing who is merrily welcoming this law! Politicians are providing explanations that this law prevents forced religious conversions based on enticements. Some people here give explanations in a manner which seeks to degrade and vulgarize the fundamental reason behind the religious conversion of Dalits which is basically their attempt to escape casteist atrocities. On that basis, it has been defined that this law is to prevent the practice of enticements and lures to carry out religious conversion.

If a person changes his religion for petty benefits, it only means that in Hinduism atrocities and oppression dominate to the extent that even such small benefits are refused! If it is said that the lay people who suffer in poverty convert their religion for ordinary comforts, then, for what did the revolutionary Dr. Ambedkar change his religion? For comforts? Is religious conversion a method that has been created yesterday or today? Even before the advent of Christianity and Islam on the Indian soil, did not religious conversion take place from Saivism to Vaishnavism and from Vaishnavism to Saivism? Today Saivism and Vaishnavism are presented as a single religion!

But are the relations between these two religions so simple? The enmity and the clashes that took place between them and the resulting influences are all imprinted in history as scars and bloodstains! Today the custom of teasing a person who has been cheated by another, by saying, *'Naamam Saathi Vittaan'* (lit. he has thrust the mark of Vishnu) is in practice. That is, it means that a Saivaite who customarily applied sacred ash across his forehead is slowly cheated and converted to Vaishnavism and the traditional symbol of the Vaishnavaite faith, the vertical mark of Vishnu, the *naamam,* is thrust on him! In this manner, why did conversions from Saivism to Vaishnavism take place? For the sake of concessions? Can anybody deny this?

From the time religions were formed, the right to convert existed, that custom was born. In violation of the Constitutional doctrine of secularism, the Tamil Nadu Government has brought the Prohibition of Religious Conversion Act only to snatch away that kind of fundamental democratic right. In this context, is the governance in Tamil Nadu to safeguard religion? Or, is it to safeguard humanity? Will this law that prohibits religious conversion, convert the mind of him who forced another man to eat excrement?

23 October 2002

v.i.c.t.o.r.y

TAMIL RULE BLOOMED IN THE VANNI FOREST!

Buddhist monks clad in saffron robes and Sinhalese people are now travelling on that highway. Like going on excursions they are constantly travelling to Jaffna in vehicles. For the past few months that highway has been opened after seven years on the basis of the Memorandum of Understanding between the Tigers and the Sinhalese Government. So the Sinhalese are going in large groups to view those affected areas and to meet their relatives stationed in the army. That road, A9, is a national highway between Kandy and Jaffna. It is opened at seven in the morning is closed again at half past five in the evening. After that time, no one can walk in those streets. It is never opened on Sundays.

After crossing Vavuniya, the territory controlled by the Sinhalese army comes to an end. There, a security fort has been established. Next to that, at a distance of 60 metres the territory of the Liberation

Tigers begins. A security fort of the Tigers has been setup there.

The land between these two is called *Shunya Pradesam* (Ground Zero). That area is under the control of the International Red Cross. When we cross it and enter the Tiger-controlled area we are able to see that a separate Government—a Tamil Government is functioning there. There, the administration of the Tigers is functioning as a Government parallel to the Sinhalese Government. From a place called Puliyangulam, Tamil Eelam Transport Corporation buses engraved with the Tiger's emblem ply. Frisking sheds have been setup, passengers (and luggage) are intensely examined and only later are they allowed to pass.

In that highway, starting from Puliyangulam, till Palai, the Government of the Tigers is functioning. The entire Killinochi and Mullaithivu districts and a few areas of the Vavuniya and Mannar districts are under the control of the Tigers. They are calling this Vanni Desam. A Tamil king, Paayum Puli Pandara Vanniyan, ruled the great stretch of this Vanni land in ancient times. It is worth mentioning that the Tigers have taken control of, and are today ruling, the same Vanni Desam. There, the respective offices of several sectors like the transportation sector, police, judiciary, finance sector, political sector, educational sector, economic development sector, agricultural sector are functioning. The administration of the Tigers can be seen in all areas like production, distribution, and tax enforcement.

Of the total area of 8000 square kilometers of the territory of Tamil Eelam, a little less than 4000 square kilometres is now under the control of the Tigers. A great portion of this is contained in Vanni Desam. Killinochi is functioning as the capital of Vanni Desam. The historically famous A9 highway traverses only through this city. Anyone who goes through that road to Jaffna and returns will understand the condition of Tamil Eelam.

After crossing Palai, which is the boundary of the Tiger-controlled area, from a place called Mugamalai the area controlled by the Sinhalese army begins. There also serious frisking takes place for hours. In this manner, one can go to Jaffna only after going through all the frisking, which the Tigers and the Sinhalese army are alternatively conducting. On both sides of that A9 highway, the lives of the Eelam Tamilians lie crushed and charred. Homes, commercial buildings, schools, temples, churches and mosques, everything lies demolished and scattered because of the rampage of the Sinhala Army.

Mr. Thilak shows two LTTE Matyrs' tombs to visiting journalists

More than everything, the skyscraping palm trees—the symbol of self-respect for the Eelam Tamilians—are all beheaded and stand as bare torsos. The palm trees are the only life supporting basic wealth of the Eelam Tamilians. For generations and generations, only the palm trees made the Tamilians live and supported and protected their lives. That type of livelihood is completely destroyed today. It is a great surprise that overcoming all the destruction and bearing all the loss, with new vigour and undiminished heroism, the Eelam Tamilians are standing in the battlefield and at the same time taking part in the reconstruction work.

Without forgetting their gratitude to all the heroes who attained martyrdom and in a manner of reminding the future generation, the people have set up here and there, *Maaveerar Thuilum Illangal* (lit. homes where the great heroes sleep). One is enthralled by the gracefulness with which these are taken care of.

We come to know that till now, 17648 Tigers have attained martyrdom. All these Tigers have been buried with complete details, and every year from 20 to 27 November is declared as Heroes Day and homage is paid. The Sinhalese army has lost three times more than the Tigers. But the Sinhalese Government does not pay such homage to the military soldiers. Instead of calling the body of the Tigers who have attained martyrdom as a 'corpse'; they are calling it as a *'vith udal'* (lit. the body which is a seed). They are sowing each body as a seed. In the midst of the war, the concern shown for such historical chronicling reveals the respect of the Tigers for sacrifice and also shows their capacity of administration that is filled with foresightedness. For the past few years when the Jaffna district was under the control of the Sinhalese army, the many *Maaveerar Thuilum Illangal* situated there, were razed to the ground by the military. In this state of affairs, using the milieu of cease-fire, the Tigers are in the process of renovating all such *Maaveerar Thuilum Illangal* which were destroyed.

Further, the children of the martyrs are all adopted and two schools called *Sencholai* and *Arivucholai* have been setup for them where they are being educated and brought up. Also, they have created savings banks here and there and through that loans are being offered for handicrafts, small-scale industries, agriculture, etc. Further, in a manner of exposing the history-fabrication scams of the Sinhalese sectarian state in the education sector, the Tigers themselves have created a new syllabus and they are teaching it to the students.

It can be seen from the art and literature of Eelam that in the manner of official language, the language of instruction, Tamil has also developed as the military language. Not only people, but even the weapons of war are given names in Tamil—this echoes in the art and literary fields. When comparing the Eelam Tamilians with the Tamilians of Tamil Nadu who are floating in an English craze, it can be realized that Eelam Tamilians have taken gigantic strides in all fields. The historically significant conference called *Maanudathin Tamizh Koodal* 2002 (Humanity's Tamil Meet 2002) was a field where this could be heralded. In that conference not only the Tamil litterateurs and media-persons, but also the Sinhalese writers and artists participated; and their declaration "The Eelam liberation struggle is a liberation struggle for the liberation of humanity" is a historic turning-point. Whether the Sinhalese Government has accepted Eelam or not, the Sinhalese people have accepted it. The testimonies of the Sinhalese artists and litterateurs serves as evidence for this. There, whether Eelam has bloomed or not; in this widespread world, in the forests of Vanni, a Tamil Government has bloomed for the Tamil race.

20 NOVEMBER 2002

d.e.t.e.r.i.o.r.a.t.i.o.n

ADMK IS NOT A PERIYAR MOVEMENT, IT IS A PERIYAVAAL* MOVEMENT

At the very beginning blows began to rain on the basis of Periyarism when it was said, "We are not opposing Brahmins, we are only opposing Brahminism." Because Periyar fiercely believed that it was not possible to retrieve social justice without uprooting Brahmin

---

* *Periyavaal* (lit. the great one) is the brahminic term in Tamil Nadu which is used to refer to the senior Kanchi Sankaracharya, as opposed to Periyar (also lit. the great one), a Tamil word, which has become synonymous with the social-justice crusader E. V. Ramasamy, known for his anti-Brahminism. Incidentally, the term 'Periyar' was bestowed on E. V. Ramasamy during a women's conference held on 12-13 November 1938.

domination, he frothed in anger and breathed fire, saying, 'if you spot a Brahmin and a snake together, leave the snake, beat the Brahmin!' From the camp of such a Periyar itself, conspiracies to root out Periyarism have started to take root.

Periyar took up instruments like denial of god, removal of superstitions in order to destroy and crumble the foundation of Brahmin domination and Brahminism. In that also, the intensity he expressed cannot be measured. He forcefully lashed out,

> 'There is no god,
> there is no god,
> there is no god at all.
> He who invented god is a fool.
> He who propagates god is a scoundrel.
> He who worships god is a barbarian.'

From this camp of Periyar, sounded the gospel of compromise: 'One community, one god.' That is, 'it cannot be said that god is not there! god is there, He is one,' the new veda sounded. Even then, in the wake of the great storm called Periyar, Brahmin domination was shaken. Its outcome was the Dravidian upsurge!

But that growth, instead of being a victory of Periyarism, once again became Brahminism's victory. Jayalalitha is only a strong evidence for that! She, who thundered in the Legislative Assembly, 'I am only a *Brahmin* woman,' is today heading a Periyar movement called the ADMK. When a Brahmin leadership has been created today, in a Dravidian party that followed Periyar—who devoted all his energies to defeat the domination of the Brahmin leadership in all fields including political power—it cannot in anyway be the victory of Periyarism.

Is the ADMK not an evidence that the Brahminic termites have gradually corroded the fire of Periyar's principles? ADMK is only a continuation of the DMK! The ADMK leadership with a Brahmin leadership has built the Brahmin compromise, for which the DMK laid the foundation stone. The Dravidian movement which won and proved its point to Rajagopalachari then, is today going on the path shown by the Sankaracharya. The Prohibition of Forceful Religious Conversions Act is only a consequence. She said with pride in the Legislative Assembly, 'I have brought in this law only following MGR's way.' She gave an explanation that MGR wished to bring in this preventive law accepting the recommendations of the Justice Venugopal Commission.[1] The heads of the Hindu mutts including the Kanchi Sankaracharya jumped in joy and welcomed this preventive law. In such a situation, Jayalalitha is making use of MGR for support because she does not want the public to consider that this law was brought about only on the instigation of such Hindutva forces.

If Jayalalitha is functioning the way MGR liked, will she also announce that she belongs to a 'Dravidian religion' like he did? MGR was a devout worshipper of Mookambikai (an ancient Dravidian mother goddess). Though he may be called a pupil of Periyar, he lived his life basically as a theist and spiritual devotee. But still, he did not like to openly proclaim himself as Hindu. He was firm in not offending the minds of the minority Christians and Muslims who loved him and had placed their trust in him. That is why, in the early 1980s when asked what religion he belonged to, he declared 'Dravidian' religion instead of 'Hindu' religion. Even if he followed the Hindu life-style, his not declaring his religion as Hindu shows his concern for the minorities. The current Chief Minister Jayalalitha, who is MGR's follower, takes the side of the majority Hindus by asking, 'Those who feel sad for the minorities in Gujarat are not feeling sad for the majority people. Why is that?'

Along with feeling and voicing for the majority, Jayalalitha will be the first leader of the Dravidian movement who extends greetings to the Hindus during Hindu festivals like Saraswathi Puja, Karthigai Deepam, etc. Is all this what MGR liked? Even though MGR did not oppose Brahmin domination or Brahmin principles like Periyar did, it is worth mentioning that he didn't show himself as a Hindu. But his follower, the current Chief Minister Jayalalitha, is proving that she is the 'Protector of the Hindus' on every occasion.

'Do minority communities mean only Muslims and Christians? Are Jains not here? Are there no Sikhs? Are there not Buddhists?'—she is raising questions like this in the Legislative Assembly itself. She is expressing her concern for the welfare of the majority Hindus to that extent. It will be correct to say that giving voice to the minority, more than being based on sympathy towards them, it is because of the concern over democracy. That is, the problem of the minorities must be approached on the basis that the protection of minorities is the protection of democracy. Accordingly, that should not be considered as opposed to the welfare of the majority. But Jayalalitha, on the basis of the understanding that actions in support of the minorities affect the welfare of the Hindu majority, has brought about this preventive law. These measures of the Chief Minister Jayalalitha reveal her extreme Hindu fanaticism. Moreover, it exposes that she is a Hindu fundamentalist.

MGR did not like to show himself as a Hindu fundamentalist; in the same way, he didn't like to show himself as a supporter of any caste. In a manner of implementing the thought of Periyar's abolition of caste, he erased caste names from the names of streets in Tamil Nadu. But his follower Jayalalitha proves with her conduct that she has exactly contradictory principles.

That is, the last time when she was the Chief Minister, when Arunachalam, a Central Minister belonging to the Dalit community boarded the flight in which she was to leave for Delhi, she got angry when she saw him, she raised a great flutter and he was made to get down from the plane. The media wrote that the then Chief Minister Jayalalitha behaved like that because he is a Dalit.

Are these types of approaches MGR's? MGR brought great change in the foundation of the society by abolishing the ancient institutions of village administration like Karnam, Maniam (that imposed taxes, collected revenue, etc.) and brought about a new method of administration under the leadership of the Village Administrative Officers. In a manner impossible to comprehend even in imagination, MGR created the opportunity for even those born in the cheris to head the village administration. Today, because of that, those belonging to the Dalit community have become Village Administrative Officers. But his follower Jayalalitha is protecting the casteist fanatics in Pappapatti and Keeripatti and is abetting the prevention of the democratic rights of the Dalits.

Icon of Self-respect and Social Justice

In Thinniyam, Dalits were forced to eat excretement and in Kaundampatti they were forced to drink urine.² But the Chief Minister did not show any seriousness in taking disciplinary proceedings on the casteist fanatics who humiliated and committed atrocities on Dalits. On the contrary she is extremely anxious to protect the Hindus and the Hindu religion.

She has brought the Hindu Religion Protection Act in the name of the Prohibition of Forcible Conversion Act only to please and encourage the casteist forces who have prohibited the Dalits from entering the temples in Koothirambakkam³ and Koogaiyur,⁴ and the Kanchi Sankaracharya who justifies their barbarism. Even if Dalits are forced to eat shit, or made to drink urine, according to this act it becomes compulsory for them to live as Hindus, forbearing all that. Today under the leadership of Jayalalitha, who is such a protector of Hindutva, a *'Periyar'* movement is successfully marching as a *'Periyavaal'* movement.

04 DECEMBER 2002

Notes

1. The Justice Venugopal Commission on inquiry was instituted by MGR, the then Chief Minister of Tamil Nadu following the Mandaikadu riots which took place in the year 1982 between Hindus and Christians in the Kanyakumari district. In these communal riots six people lost their lives because of police firing. The Mandaikadu riots are generally viewed as an aftermath of the religious conversion in the southern districts. In March 1981, the Dalit village of Meenakshipuram turned into Rahmat Nagar as most of the Dalit population embraced Islam; months later, the village of Uttarakosamangai in the Ramanathapuram district turned into Mohammadiapuram.

    In the report of the Justice Venugopal Commission submitted in 1986, a ban on conversion by 'fraudulent and foul means' had been recommended. But the same Commission of Inquiry had also lashed out against the Rashtriya Swayamsevak Sangh (RSS) and had called for a ban on their 'drills and parades' that created 'fear and insecurity' among the minority communities.

2. In the village of Kaundampatti in the Dindigul district, a Dalit Sankan was forced to drink urine by upper caste fanatics because of a fifteen-year long land dispute between him and members of an oppressor caste. Sankan had been a bonded laborer for thirty years. In this incident that took place on 5 September 2002, Sankan was beaten, his hands were tied and a barbaric caste-Hindu Annadurai urinated into his mouth. Annadurai is a police officer who works with the armed forces at Chennai. Earlier, on 21 May 2002, two Dalits, Ramasamy and Murugesan, were forced to consume human faeces because they dared to express their dissent against the caste-Hindus (See article '*They* Are Superior to Humans', pp. 119-22. As this book goes to press, the latest atrocity in this order has taken place: On 22 September 2003, a 38-year-old Dalit woman, Muthumari, was forced by a mob of caste-Hindu Thevars to drink excrement mixed with water in front of her husband and children because she had spurned the advances of Raju, a Thevar man in the Keela Urappanur village in Thirumangalam block in Madurai district.

r.e.v.o.l.t

Change of Name

NOT JUST A RETRIEVAL OF LANGUAGE, BUT OF HISTORY

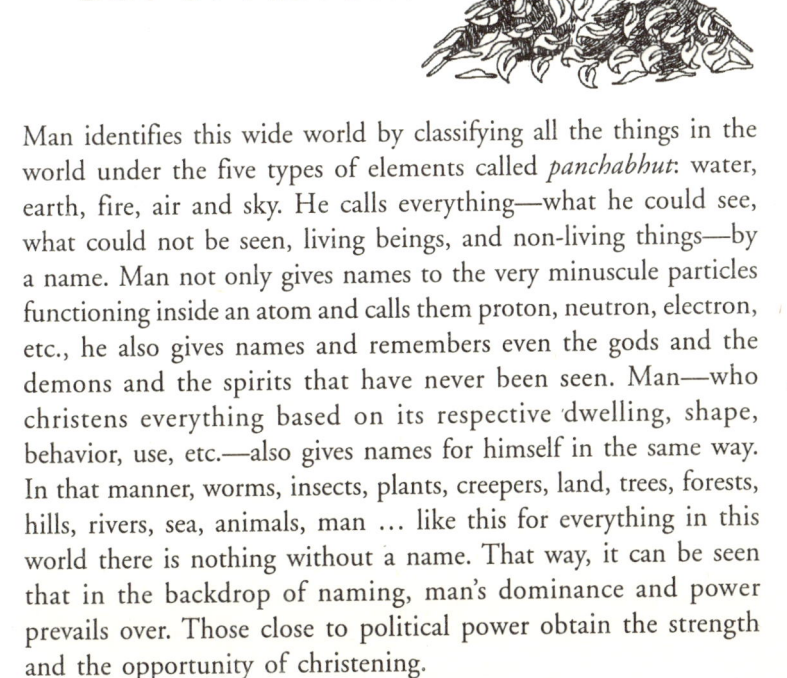

Man identifies this wide world by classifying all the things in the world under the five types of elements called *panchabhut*: water, earth, fire, air and sky. He calls everything—what he could see, what could not be seen, living beings, and non-living things—by a name. Man not only gives names to the very minuscule particles functioning inside an atom and calls them proton, neutron, electron, etc., he also gives names and remembers even the gods and the demons and the spirits that have never been seen. Man—who christens everything based on its respective dwelling, shape, behavior, use, etc.—also gives names for himself in the same way. In that manner, worms, insects, plants, creepers, land, trees, forests, hills, rivers, sea, animals, man ... like this for everything in this world there is nothing without a name. That way, it can be seen that in the backdrop of naming, man's dominance and power prevails over. Those close to political power obtain the strength and the opportunity of christening.

The mother tongue of those who have such power gets the

opportunity of being the language of christening. Today, only in that manner in the Indian soil, the English, Arabic and Sanskrit languages exert their influence in everything related to governance. But the position of Tamil language, which is praised as an ancient and classical language, has become a subject of mockery. In the Tamil land, the feeling of considering it a disgrace to give Tamil titles to Tamil movies shot in the Tamil language is rampant. *Run, King, Five Star, Youth, Gentleman, Student Number One,* . . . like this, Tamil movies are named in English. In the whole world, the mental state of considering it disgusting to name in their mother tongue, not only movies, but even humans, is rampant only among the Tamilians. Tamilians are naming themselves as Ajay, Vijay, Ramesh, Suresh, with words in northern languages that cannot be understood. The Tamilian considers it a matter of pride to write his initials (first letter of father's name) in English. To that level, English hegemony is rampant in Tamil Nadu. The mind of the Tamilian has been spoilt to the extent that he considers it as 'low' to keep names in Tamil.

The basis for Tamil becoming a victim (to this extent) is that the rulers and the Tamil people consider themselves more as 'Hindus' than as Tamilians. At no point of time, will a Tamilian who thinks of himself as a Hindu consider Tamil and Tamil nationalism as important. On the contrary, he will consider Sanskrit and Hindutva as his breath. A Tamilian who upholds Sanskrit and Hindutva can never prevent casteism and its effects. It can be clearly seen that Tamil and the Tamil race are destroyed because of casteism and Hindutva. Realizing this, Tamil scholars and leaders of the Dravidian movement opposed Brahmin domination. Tamil scholars like Maraimalai Adigal, Devaneya Pavanar, Perunchithiranar took up the struggle against Sanskritic supremacy. They changed all the Sanskrit names and gave themselves Tamil names. On that basis only, the Tamil scholar Vedachalam changed his name to Maraimalai and Surya Narayana Shastri became Parithimar Kalaignar, etc. The upsurge of such an independent Tamil movement opposed to Sanskritic hegemony continued till the beginning of the Dravidian

A section of people who took names in Tamil at the Viduthalai Chiruthaigal Function on Dr. Ambedkar's death anniversary, 06 Dec 2002

movement.

After that, instead of evolving into a people's movement it stagnated. The fundamental reason for this stagnation was they took up the opposition of Brahminism and Sanskrit instead of dropping the Hindutva life-style. A Hindu can oppose Brahmin-Sanskrit domination to a specific limit, but he cannot continue after that. That is, a non-Brahmin Hindu can oppose a Brahmin Hindu; he cannot oppose Hindutva. The opposition to Hindutva means, it must cross the Brahmin boundary and spread till the non-Brahmin caste-Hindus. How can a Hindu take forward such a Hindutva opposition? Because the non-Brahmin non-Dalit caste-Hindus believe themselves to be Hindus, they accept the Brahmin-Sanskrit culture itself as their culture and carry the burden of Hindu names. For ages and ages, the same situation is being deviously imposed on the Dalit people also. The oppressed Buddhists who resisted and fiercely opposed the Hindutva caste structure are today imprisoned in the prison of the cheri. Being afraid of the state atrocities and rampages by the Hindu religion, which was anti-

Buddhist and anti-Jainist, the people who obeyed and surrendered were accepted as 'shudra' and they were classified as caste-Hindus. So, today's shudra and Dalit people are basically not Hindus. Contrarily, Hindutva was imposed on them.

That is why, revolutionary Dr. Ambedkar exposed to the nation the historical truth—'Dalits are not Hindus.' But to show that Hindus are the majority in India, the Dalit people were also joined in the census as Hindus. Recorded evidence is available that in the population census taken in 1910 they were not classified as Hindus, instead they were separately classified. That itself serves as evidence that Dalits do not belong to the Hindu religion.

As a result of the imposition of Hindutva identity, using power and privilege to permeate in the cultural field, on a society that was non-Hindu, today unknown to their own selves the Dalits wander with the burden of Hindu names. But, even now they have not been accepted as Hindus. Christians can enter churches, Muslims can enter the mosques, and Hindus can enter into temples. But the cheri people who are called Hindus are not permitted to enter any temple in the village.

The Koogaiyur Ayyanar temple

Koothirambakkam,[1] Koogaiyur,[2] Azhagapuram,[3] in any village, Dalits are not allowed to enter Hindu temples. Why is that? Apart from the reason that they are basically not Hindus, the fundamental reason is that for ages and ages they have retaliated against Hindutva!

From the time Hindu rule was established in this land Buddhism and Jainism have not been allowed to raise their heads. Their annihilation and destruction was plotted, and to make it permanent the practice of untouchability was conveniently created

Thirumaavalavan addresses a massive Viduthalai Chiruthaigal protest meeting in Koogaiyur for a temple-entry agitation on 16 Nov 2002

and followed continuously from generation to generation. Apart from those who embraced Christianity and Islam, opposing that kind of disgrace, the state atrocity of not allowing the remaining people to quit the Hindu classification is today's Prohibition of Forcible Religious Conversion Act.[4] Basically, this law will be fit to be termed as the 'Hindu Religion Protection Act'. When the Government itself forces the Dalit people to live as Hindus through this law, it is a historical compulsion for the Dalit people to agitate not only against this law but against Hindutva itself. In that manner, to establish that they are not Hindus is it not a necessity for the Dalit people to shed the Hindu names which they are carrying unawares? As an alternative, taking excellent Tamil names which are devoid of caste and religion identity is a way of Hindutva opposition.[5] In the whole world, only Tamil and the Tamil race

Viduthalai Chiruthaigal cadres burning copies of the 'Prohibition of Forcible Conversion Act'

are secular, i.e., they don't have any religious affiliation. Abdullah indicates Islam, Antony indicates Christianity, Ariharan shows Hindutva, Ajay Singh shows a Sikh identity.

But the Tamil name Arivazhagan (lit. beautiful in intelligence) does it show any religion identity? Even though Hindus might

Thirumaavalavan thunders to lakhs of Tamilians in a Viduthalai Chiruthaigal ceremony to take names in Tamil held on 14 April 2003 (Dr. Ambedkar's birth anniversary) at Madurai

own such names, it is not true that they are Hindu names. Only Tamil names do not have caste or religious identity. So changing Hindu names to Tamil names will cause a retrieval of the Tamil language and Tamil race and will also cause secularism to be safeguarded and the abolition of caste would also be taken up. The question may arise as to what revolutionary change is going to take place because of changing of names. Change of names is not a symbol particular to the language alone, it is a symbol of retrieval of history. That is why, when Mustafa Kamal Pasha restructured Turkey, he changed not only the names of the people, but he changed even the names of the places there. In the world today the names of several different countries have been changed only on that basis. Recently, Burma became Myanmar, likewise in India,

Bombay became Mumbai, Calcutta became Kolkata, and Madras became Chennai only on this basis. So change of name is not just the retrieval of identity or language, it is the retrieval of a race's history.

25 DECEMBER 2002

Notes

1. The Dalit people of the Koothirambakkam village in the Kanchipuram district have been demanding, for over three decades, that the deity of the Muthumari amman temple in the village (which is controlled by the caste-Hindu Vanniyars) should also come to the cheri when it is taken in a procession around the village. The Vanniyars—who openly follow untouchability—say that the deity is not taken to the cheri because it would get 'polluted'. They don't allow the Dalits inside the temple, into caste-Hindu village areas, or to draw water from the village pond. Because Dalits demanded their right to enter the temple, they were denied jobs on caste-Hindu lands and were economically boycotted. They announced that no one of them should talk to Dalits, and those violating this are fined two thousand rupees. When Dalits tried to fish in the pond based on a lease granted to them by the district administration, they were attacked with sickles and sticks and chased back to the cheri. Eighteen Dalits including women and children were hurt in the attack and had to be hospitalized. The caste-Hindus ransacked fifty houses of the Dalits, looted and damaged property.

    It is also a matter worthy of note, that of the more than ten temples in the village, the Dalits demand entry only into the Muthumari amman temple, because they had contributed money towards its construction. Every year peace-meetings were held, but the demands of the Dalits would be rejected. In September 2002, the Dalits announced their decision to convert to Islam right in front of the Kanchipuram mutt and put up banners. In order to sidetrack the prominent issue and to appease Dalits, the Government departments provided civic amenities to the cheri: an 'exclusive' overhead tank, pipe water from the tank in the main village, four hand-pumps (which were given in order to nullify the Dalits' demand for rights to the common village pond), nine-street lights, a drainage scheme and forty-eight group houses.

2. For over eighty years, Dalits have not been allowed to enter the Veera Baiyankara Ayyanar temple in the village of Koogaiyur near Kallakurichi in the Villupuram district in Tamil Nadu. The temple enjoys a steady and high revenue because it is famous for its black magic. The temple owns

forty-five acres of land. The Dalits demanded entry into the temple just to look at the Ayyanar's face; they had not demanded anything big, say, a share in the temple revenue or land. Even their demand for temple entry was rebuffed. On 11 November 2002 a conciliation team met, they sought a time frame of five days from the rebelling Dalits. In the meantime, the priests of the temple moved court and obtained a stay order refraining 'outsiders' from entering the temple. On 16 November 2002, Thirumaavalavan visited Koogaiyur and addressed a gathering of thousands of Dalits (see photograph p. 161). He cautioned that such a large number of Dalits could enter the temple, and it would be impossible for the people of the village or the police there from stopping their entry. Following this, on 10 December 2002, Dalits were able to finally enter the Ayyanar temple at Koogaiyur along with the Governmental authorities though the caste-Hindus and the priests were opposed to it.

3. See note no.6, p.9 for the temple-entry in Azhagapuram.
4. The Prohibition of Forcible Conversion of Religion Ordinance was promulgated as an Emergency Act on 5 October 2002, when the Assembly was to meet in twenty days. The Ordinance was passed as a Bill on 31 October 2002. Among those who welcomed this law were Kanchi Sankaracharya and the Hindu Munnani, a fundamentalist group. The Viduthalai Chiruthaigal considers this law anti-Dalit, for it forces Dalits to accept casteist crimes without seeking refuge in other religions, so it undertook a statewide agitation to burn copies of this law. The Act has stringent penalty measures for those 'forcibly' converting Dalits: a fine of one lakh rupees and up to four years of imprisonment.
5. Opposing the Prohibition of Forcible Conversion of Religion Act of the Tamil Nadu Government, on 6 December 2002 the memorial day of the revolutionary Dr. Ambedkar, the Viduthalai Chiruthaigal led by Thirumaavalavan put forth the slogan, 'We shall change the Hindu names; we shall take names in beautiful Tamil'; and in a function organized that day in Chennai, the list of changed names of 5115 persons was released. But as the function proceeded, the response was overwhelming and more than 8000 people changed their Sanskritic names and took names in Tamil.

In this historic function, Thirumaavalavan changed the name of his father, Ramasamy, as Tholkappian (after the ancient Tamil scholar and grammarian). So his own name R. Thirumaavalavan was changed as Thol. Thirumaavalavan. All the changed names have been legally notified and announced in the state gazette also. Subsequently, on 14 April 2003 at the birth anniversary function of Dr. Ambedkar organized by the Viduthalai Chiruthaigal at Madurai, more than 10800 people were given new Tamil names by Thirumaavalavan.

a.s.s.i.m.i.l.a.t.i.o.n

ARE SAIVISM AND VAISHNAVISM HINDU RELIGIONS?

Kudamuzhakku (lit. consecration ceremony of a temple) or prayers to god must not be offered in Tamil! Because Tamil is not a divine language, it is a low language! Voices like this which degrade Tamil language and the Tamil race are not heard somewhere else, in a corner of the European or Arabian countries! Contrarily, this is being spoken against the Tamil language and against the Tamil race in the Tamil land itself, that too in the Tamil language itself without any bit of hesitation or fear, by those very people who eat the salt of the Tamilians. Today, this is the disgraceful position of the historically famous Tamil itself, which is the world's ancient language and which is an exalted classical language. Recently near Karur, there has been a prohibition to perform the *Kudamuzhakku* for the Manimutheeswarar temple in the Tamil language! As a direct reaction of the prohibition of worship in Tamil, the Tamil feeling, which for a long time was in ashes, has now started to spread as a fire.

The war cry, 'We will worship Tamil, we will worship in Tamil alone', has erupted in Karur today. The historical truth that Saivism and Vaishnavism are Tamil religions and they are not Hindu religions has come to light.

Things like the Aryan Brahminism, Varnashrama Dharma, Manu Dharma—none of them are doctrines or code of ethics of the Tamilians! The Indus Valley and Harappa civilizations are evidence that in the cultural field, even thousands of years ago the Tamilians lived elegantly in a manner that surprised the entire world. Specially, in the spiritual field too, the Tamil race guided humanity as a model! It was the tradition of the Tamil race to erect and worship a *nadukal* (memorial stone) in honor of the leaders who protected and guided the clan members after their death! Today also, in a few places in villages the custom of erecting *nadukal* is still in practice.

Hindutva and Aryanism/Sanskrit are all founded on *puranas*, on myths. Contrarily, the spirituality of the Tamilians is founded on history. The worship of memorial stones by the Tamil race serves as evidence. Even now, the stories of the *siru-deivangal* (lit. small gods—but here it refers to non-brahminical godheads) in the villages, instead of being imaginatively concocted and tall stories of fiction, are in tandem with the natural life-style of those people who worship these gods. Tamilians have prayed to people who have lived amidst people as human beings, as *Andavan* (deity) or *Iraivan* (presiding deity). The phrases among Tamilians like *Andavan, Iraivan, koil,* etc., make it clear that they prayed to and worshipped their respective clan leaders after their death. Does not *Andavan* and *Iraivan* mean king and does *koil* not mean home of the ruler?

The Tamilians have followed the unadulterated culture of worshipping small gods by erecting *nadukal* for one who was either a king or ruler of a clan and by calling him as *Andavan* and the place of worship as *koil*. In the course of time, because of the several invasions, which took place on the Tamilians, cultural intermingling occurred and because of the dominance exerted by the Sanskrit-Aryan Hinduism, the worship of avatars was established. Because of this, the entire Tamil racial identity was crushed. Though the language is Tamil, the Tamilians only lead their lives as Hindu. Only in this situation, if anyone disgraces or blames the Tamil language or the Tamil race, the Tamilian doesn't get angry. The Tamilian, instead of *being* a Tamilian, lives as a Hindu who solely stands against the growth of the Tamil language and the Tamil people. The Tamilian and Tamil language who once ruled from the throne, have now been pushed to the disgraceful position of 'untouchable'. That is why, even the Tamilian who lives as a Hindu is prohibited from entering the sanctum sanctorum of a temple. Even the Tamil language has been prohibited entry into the sanctum

Thirumaavalavan with heads of Saiva mutts during the 'Conference on Worship in Tamil' held at Karur in Dec 2002

sanctorum. So it is the law of the Hindutva that there is no place for Tamil and Tamilians in the sanctum sanctorum of the temples. The Tamilian who opposed this cruel law is the *panchama*. The Tamilian who accepted it is the *shudra*!

While the panchama is not allowed to enter the temple, the shudra is not allowed to enter the sanctum sanctorum. More than the Tamilian not being allowed to enter the sanctum sanctorum, it is of primary importance that the Tamil mother, who gave birth to that Tamilian son, is herself not allowed to enter into the sanctum sanctorum. When the mother herself doesn't have a position, how will the son get a place? If the disgrace of Mother Tamil and Tamil people not being permitted entry into the temple must be abolished, each and every Tamilian must realize that he is not a Hindu. Even if he lives spiritually as a Saivaite or as a Vaishnavaite, he must basically realize the historical truth that he is not a Hindu with the Aryan-Sanskrit life-style.

The Tamilians followed the worship of small gods like Ayyanar, Veeranar, Maariyaayi, Karuppusamy, Muniyandi and the worship of larger godheads like Sivan, Thirumal and Murugan have lost their power and rulership because of the cultural invasion of the Aryan Hindutva. Saivism and Vaishnaivism which were nurtured by the ancient Tamilians at that time, have been swallowed by the

Hindutva. The Aryan supremacy that Sanskrit alone is the language understood by god has prevailed over. On that basis only, Tamil was blamed as being a 'low' language. Centuries ago, an ethical struggle to worship god in Tamil itself started in Tamil Nadu protesting against this type of Aryan domination. Saints like Vadalur Vallalar stood in the forefront of such an ethical struggle. As a continuation, in Karur the battle drums for that ethical war have started to sound.

Covered with ashes but still containing the fire, the ash-smeared Saiva heads of mutts and the Vaishnava holy seers have all donned the war form. By taking up the gauntlet to protect the right of worship in Tamil, all the Saiva mutts like the Madurai Adheenam, Kundrakudi Adheenam, Thiruvanamalai Adheenam, Thiruvaduthurai Adheenam, have exposed to the Tamil race that they are not Hindutva. They have made it evident that Aryanism and Sanskrit alone are the basis of Hindutva. In those times, Thirugnanasambandar was identified by the Adi Sankara as a 'Dravidian child' for having worshipped Siva in Tamil in opposition to this. Only because of that even today in Brahmin households children are not named as Thirugnanasambandar. It becomes evident that Saivism and Tamil were considered as enemy by Aryans to that extent.

In this situation how can Saivism or Vaishnavism be Hinduism? Whether spirituality is necessary or not for humanity, let that be on one side! In today's condition, it is of primary significance whether Hindutva means friend or foe for Tamil and Tamilians. In this context, it is the duty of every Tamilian to retrieve/redeem the Tamil language and race by winning over the forces that accuse and oppose the Tamil language and Tamil race, however strong they may be. In that way, to safeguard the right of worship in Tamil, the Siva Adigalars covered in holy ash have donned a war form. The Tamil language or the Tamil race can never be retrieved if this ethical battle contracts into a battle against the Brahmins alone. It must expand into a righteous struggle against Hindutva that is founded on the Varnashrama Dharma! Only then, in the sanctum sanctorum of the temple, in the fort, in the throne, the rule of Mother Tamil will flower again!

22 JANUARY 2003

s.t.r.u.g.g.l.e

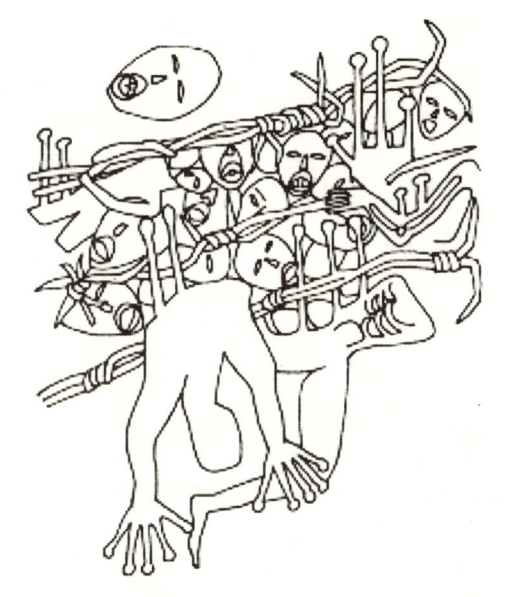

MUST VENMANI BE FENCED?

There were not glossy red flags in their hands, but rugged cudgels! On their hips, they had not the sickles to reap crop, but sickles to slit throats! In their eyes was not to be seen the comradeship of the proletariat, but furious fascist dominance!... Who are they, who exposed themselves in such a form in the village of Venmani?

They are the revolutionaries who have come to plant communism in this world! They are the heroes of the Red Army who came to destroy the arrogance of feudalism that declared, 'I am everything, everything is for me!' They are the Marxists who came to control the insolence of exploiters and establish a Government of the proletariat!

They became like this?...

'The title-deed for the Venmani memorial is in our name, it is our property!'—Is such a loud and lofty capitalist voice emanating

The Venmani memorial

from these communists? 'No one else should come to the Venmani memorial; we alone will celebrate functions; we alone will pay our respects'—Saying so, Marxists have raised a wall around Venmani and they are enjoying the sole rights to the property for the past thirty years! Is this perhaps the democracy of the proletariat?...

Any distortionist of history cannot hide the fact that when the farm labourers united against the dominance of the casteist feudalism's atrocities, which included practices like forceful ingestion of cow-dung solution, whipping, etc., they were guided by the 'Marxists' who stood in the forefront of the struggle. In such a situation, it is a great shock to realize that they are trapped in the quagmire of capitalism: they suppose that they are enjoying the ownership of history by owning the 'memorial' property. It is agonizing that those who once hoisted the red flag and thundered out seeking to demolish any type of hegemony and reactionary conduct are today the victims of the same cancerous supremacist feeling and backward-looking character.

'Those who were in this party must not go to another; those

who gripped this flag, must not hold another'—if such a kind of democracy is being adopted by a Marxist party itself, to what kind of list can we add this type of conduct? If those who had carried the Marxist red flag, even held another red flag, they are segregated from the village, their property is plundered, they are massacred and similar violent and rampageous conduct occurs in many villages in the Tanjore area. It is the practice even today! How many scars and bloodstains serve as reminders even now! Is democracy, this kind of denial and prevention of the individual liberty to choose? This is called Fascism!

What is the difference between telling someone, 'Don't enter the temple' and 'Don't enter into the Venmani memorial?' This is only a harvest of the regressive school of thought that claims, 'This

A section of the audience in the Viduthalai Chiruthaigal meeting held at Tanjore commemorating the Venmani massacre anniversary

is mine!' This is only an expression of feudalism that says, 'I alone have the right to exercise power and dominance over this!' Not only for the Viduthalai Chiruthaigal but even for the senior communist parties the gates were not opened till the past four-five years: Why is that? Even if we accept for argument's sake, the contention of these 'Marxists' that the entry of the Viduthalai Chiruthaigal into Venmani will produce a 'casteist stain' in the history of the Venmani struggle, why are the other friendly communist parties, that do not have any caste label, denied entry? Is it Marxist democracy to ban and isolate the forces of comradeship among the proletariat?

Viduthalai Chiruthaigal members marching to the Venmani memorial on 25 Dec 2002

The Marxists recorded this earth-shattering brutal massacre in history as a 'class struggle' alone! Why was the integrated 'casteist supremacy' covered up? Even though the struggle for increased wages took place between the proletariat represented by the farm-labourers and the bourgeois represented by the landlords, all the forty-four people who were burned and charred in the slums set afire by Gopalakrishna Naidu's gang were Dalits. Why is it that there is not a single Kallar or Vanniyar worker among the victims? Perhaps the proletariat had agitated without any difference between Kallar and Pallar. But only with the violent fury of casteist dominance did the exploitative bourgeois Naidu's gang reduce to ashes the cheri in Venmani! Instead of exposing this type of casteism, why has it been established as a class conflict? Even if the Marxists do not have a casteist approach, must not the casteist arrogance of Naidu's gang be revealed? For that mob to set fire to the cheris, is feudalistic dominance the reason? Or is casteist arrogance the reason?

Although the failure to expose the casteist activities of Naidu's gang of hooligans may not be a schemed act; it only means that the 'Marxists' collaborated to cover up the tendency of casteist supremacy existing within the proletariat! The 'Marxists' do not want to oppose or contradict the caste-Hindu workers by supporting the Dalit workers. That is why 'Marxists' are not able to develop an independent action-plan to seriously struggle when direct atrocities of casteist rampage like Melavalavu, Pappapatti or Thinniyam take place.

The screams of the forty-four people burnt alive stilled the world for a moment, but it was not possible for the Marxists to get even one day of jail sentence for the murderous Gopalakrishna Naidu! In fact, only the affected workers and a few individuals, who understood Marxism and Leninism from them, showed concern for the acquittal of the brutal murderer Naidu by the ruling class. They alone avenged this and rewrote the judgment! Do the Marxists who have put up a fence around Venmani, have any role in this chronicled history?

Without allowing anybody, they are showing interest merely in celebrating every year, the 'Class Unity: Venmani Day.' What is the difference between following the ritual of death anniversary and the celebration of 'Venmani Day?' 'Class unity,' means the unity of which class? What does it show when forces of the proletariat like the Viduthalai Chiruthaigal were attacked with cudgels, were shoved by their necks and were chased away saying, 'What is your business here?' It simply shows that the unity of the working class has charred as the forty-fifth corpse along with the forty-four heroes! It also shows that Gopalakrishna Naidu is yet to die! Moreover, does it not display that what they desire is not the unity of the proletariat!

If capitalist thought and supremacist rage are so rampant even in those who claim to have studied Marxism, why will it not be present in those like Gopalakrishna Naidu?

The casteist, feudalistic, bourgeois and capitalist forces cannot digest any progressive change! It is not a matter of surprise! On the contrary, if conflicting thoughts prevail in those who have studied Marxist dialectics relating to 'change', they can only be the heirs of Naidu; how can they be the followers of Marxism?

12 FEBRUARY 2003

Notes

> **VICTIMS**: Paapa (25), Chandra (12), Aasai Thambi (10), Vasuki (3), Sundaram (45), Saroja (12), Vasuki (5) Marudhammal (25), Thangaiyan (5), Chinnapillai (25), Karunanidhi (12), , Kunjammal (30), Poomayil (16), Karupaayee (35), Rajee Ammal (16), Damodharam (12), Jeyam (10), Rasendran (7), Subban (70), Kuppammal (60), Packiam (35), Jothi (10), Kalimuthu (35), Gurusamy (15), Natarajan (5), Virammal (22), Pattu (46), Shanmugam (13), Vedavalli (10), Kanagammbal (25).
>
> *And 14 persons of one family:* Kadumbayee (50), Kaveri (50), Anjalai (45), Murugan (45), Murugan (40), Srinivasan (40), Srinivasan (38), Aachee ammal (30), Sethu (26), Nagarajan (10), Jayam (6), Natarajan (6), Selvi (3) and Andal (2).

1. The village of Kila Venmani is situated in the highly fertile erstwhile Tanjore district of Tamil Nadu. In the 1960s, most of the lands in this district were distributed only among a few major landlords: Poondi Vandayar, Ukkadai Thevar, Vadapathimangalam Thyagaraja Mudaliar, Kuniyur Sambasiva Iyer, Pattukottai Naadimuthu Pillai and people of the Naidu caste. When the farm-labourers formed an association, these landlords formed a Paddy Producers' Association for which they enrolled goondas.

Gopalakrishna Naidu, a rich landlord who owned the Venmani village, was selected President. Whenever the labourers organized themselves and demanded more wages, they were cruelly punished, whipped and forced to drink excrement mixed with water. The Venmani carnage that took place on 25 December 1968—where forty-four cheri persons, including sixteen men (ten of them under sixteen) and twenty-eight women (twelve of them under sixteen) were killed—was not the first instance of its kind, but it was the gravest tragedy. Many had lost their lives because of the feudal arrogance of the landlords. As the labourers continued to agitate— pathetically, the increase demanded was merely a kilo of paddy—this struggle continued, and eight people were murdered. This resulted in a more vigorous agitation by the proletariat.

In December 1968, Muthusamy, a Marxist party cadre was kidnapped by Gopalakrishna Naidu and locked up in some home. The cheri people came to know about this and rescued Muthusamy. This was the immediate provocation. The caste-fanatic Naidu went along with the police and his hoodlums and attacked the cheri. The cheri people retaliated and one of his gang members died. This infuriated him more and he set fire to the cheri. People fled and some of them took shelter in a hut. He locked the hut and set fire to it, preventing the trapped people any escape. In that gruesome mass-lynching that took place on 25 December 1968, forty-four people were brutally burnt to death. When this issue was raised in the Legislative Assembly, the then Chief Minister Annadurai asked people to forget it as though it were a bad dream, a flash of lightning. It is a scar on the Indian judicial system that Gopalakrishna Naidu did not spend a single day in jail for this horrifying cruelty. Although the lower court ordered ten years of imprisonment, the Madras High Court set free all the accused on the conjecture that it was not possible for a big landlord to do like that.

e.x.p.l.o.i.t.a.t.i.o.n

IS THE TAMIL LAND INFERTILE AND FALLOW?

Has the fertile land of Tamil Nadu which was replete and dense with flourishing natural resources, lost its shape and become a dry desert where poverty and diseases are rampant?

Today, the Tamil Nadu Government has given its statement of confession that even if there is not clean water to quench the thirst, with the exception of the capital Chennai, the entire land is parched, wrecked and maimed. Is the Tamil land so infertile and fallow that to manage and withstand the cruelty of the drought and the malady of poverty, it must seek the monetary help of the Central Government to lavishly give it several thousand crores? In the fertile land of Tanjore of which has been said, 'oxen did not suffice to thresh but elephants were needed'—in that historically famous land of the Cholas, today, snails are boiled and sucked, little rats are roasted and eaten to satisfy the hunger of the Tamilians. Why has this situation been created? This is a humiliation for the Tamil land and the Tamil race!

A school-going child, Prakash of Aadhichapuram, became a prey to the cruel hunger of starvation. Is this starvation death taking place in Tanjore that is the source of paddy for the entire Tamil Nadu? Following that, how many lives of Tamilians have become mouthfuls of food for the wide-mouthed hunger of drought that is on the rampage! What is the reason for this type of cruel drought and poverty? Who is responsible? Can the blame be laid on nature, saying, 'There wasn't sufficient rainfall, therefore drought sprouted and poverty branched and spread?' Is it right? Who can deny that the basis for this malady of drought, is that Cauvery which made the Tamil soil fertile was blocked. The political policy is the basic reason! To protect and maintain the fertility and lushness of the Kannada soil, the rulers of Karnataka are sucking the very blood of Cauvery.

At any point of time they have never obeyed the orders of the Cauvery River Tribunal or the Arbitration Panel or even the Supreme Court judgment. Even within the territory of the Indian Government, Karnataka has never once given up its individual right as a state! But are the political policies and stands of the rulers of Tamil Nadu for the self-determination of Tamil Nadu? More than the fertility of the Tamil land, more than the well being of the Tamil people, for the Tamil Nadu politicians, India and the Indian national consciousness is primary! The Dravidian parties like the DMK, ADMK have extra Indian patriotism even more the Congress Party in Tamil Nadu! They may give up the rights of the Tamil people, but they will never give up Indian national integration! Not only among the Tamil parties, but even among the Tamil people such a feeling prevails.

The mental state has grown to the extent that the Tamil national feeling itself is considered as an 'anti-national' crime. The water resources of the Tamil land are sucked, its mineral resources are exploited, and the Tamil parties and the Tamil people are not bothered about it. They are not even a little worried that deviously the flourishing of their language and the racial well-being are destroyed.

That is why, not only Kannadigas but even Malayalees today have entered the field to destroy Tamil Nadu's water resources. In a place called Mukkali, a dam is being built across the Bhavani River. They are involved in efforts to completely dry up the western districts including Coimbatore, Erode, Salem. They do not obey the Central Government's orders. The Kerala Government also did not comply

Is the Tamil Land Infertile and Fallow?

with the talks held with Tamil Nadu ministers and officials. If the Kannadigas are expressing their inability to give the Cauvery water, the Malayalees in Bhavani's Mukkali are blocking and colonizing the river. Today, the Kannadigas and the Malayalees build dams across the rivers of Tamil Nadu. The Kerala Government has stopped the Tamil Nadu Government from increasing the height of the Mullai Periyar dam from 40 metres and 80 centimetres to 45 metres 60 centimetres by declaring its resistance and opposing the plan; and through that is destroying the lushness of the Theni and the Madurai districts. Although experts have stressed that the water-storage capacity must be increased because water is not sufficient for irrigation; for several years the Kerala Government is preventing the increase by not permitting the rise. But why could the Tamil Nadu Government not prevent the Kerala Government from building a dam across the Bhavani River, at a place where no dam existed earlier?

Not only in rivers and dams, but even in temples the rights of the Tamilians are being snatched away. For long, the Kerala Government has prohibited Tamilians inside the Kannagi temple. The Tamilians who were deprived of their land in the border areas today stand in despair as they have lost the entire land of Tamil Nadu to the plundering by the non-Tamilians. The Indian nation plunders and exploits the extensive mineral resources present underground. By looting the material resources flourishing on the land, the gang of non-Tamilians, the north-Indian migrants fatten. The daylight robbery gang called the multinational corporations sucks all the labour of the factory workers, the farm labourers and the rest of the proletariat! Thus, the Tamil land and the Tamil race are hunted upon in several angles.

In the cultural field also, Hindutva which imposes Aryan hegemony is completely destroying the identity of the Tamilians. The Tamilian has been made into a victim of the mental disease of inferiority complex to the extent that he considers it disgraceful to think and talk in Tamil. That is why in Tamil Nadu, in the temples built by the Tamilians, non-Tamilians dare to tell that there is no place for Tamilians. They are able to degrade Tamilians as the 'sons-of-whores' and they call Tamil a *neecha baasha* (lit. low language).

That is why in English schools the unrestrained behaviour of the Anglophiles goes to the extent of punishing children speaking in Tamil. It is possible for the ruling coterie to cackle, 'It is not compulsory for the Governor's speech to be read in Tamil.' How can this become a practice in Tamil Nadu? The basic reason for the casteless religionless sons-of-the-soil Tamilians—who belong to a race that lived as a pioneer for the world's human race itself in all fields—to be made into Hindus, into Indians, is because their power has been castrated. The burdensome Sanskrit, English and Arabic names they carry serve as an evidence that the Tamilians who were deprived of all prosperity, well-being and living right; and stand lost of power and identity. They consider it a humiliation to keep Tamil names itself!

Is it just the names of individuals? Like the Tamilian, the names of villages, the names of streets, the names of Gods, names of temples have all lost their Tamil identity! 'Kudamukku' has become Kumbakonam; and 'Thirumaraikaadu' has become Vedaranyam and 'Thirumudhukundram' has become Virudhachalam and Mamallapuram has become 'Mahabalipuram'; like this many names of places are deprived of their Tamil identity.

The Peruvudayar temple in Tanjore became the Brihadeeswarar temple, and Annamalaiar temple in Thiruvanamalai became the Arunchaleshwar temple; like this many names of temple and gods have lost the Tamil identity. To lose identity means losing dominance. The one who loses both dominance and identity will also be forced to lose power and governance. Instead of losing his rights to live and rights to livelihood as a consequence; what else can he do? Only on that basis, the Kannadigas and Malayalees build dams over Cauvery and Bhavani and deny water! In this condition, Tamilians will furtively ask help from Kannadigas, Malayalees and Telugus —what else is the way? Apart from kneeling before the superpower of the Central Government, what else is the solution?

The only path is in the retrieval of the identity, individuality and authority that the Tamilians have lost regrettably! The only potent medicine for that retrieval is the Tamil nationalism that says, 'Tamil Nadu is for the Tamilians alone.'

26 February 2002

i.n.d.e.x

A9 highway, 147-49
Abdul Kalam, 115-18
Afghanistan, 21
Anna Dravida Munnetra Kazhagam (ADMK), xix-xx, xxvi, 15-18, 34, 40, 85-88, 97-100, 110-11, 118, 125-26, 137, 145, 151-55, 176. *See also* Jayalalitha; M. G. Ramachandran
Annadurai, 94, 174
aryan, 44, 138, 168
Ayodhya issue, 82
Azhagapuram temple, 3, 8, 160. *See also* temple-entry

Bahujan Samaj Party (BSP), xvi-xvii, 118
Balasingham Anton, 70-71. *See also* Liberation
Bharatiya Janata Party (BJP), xvi-xvii, 40, 90, 99, 116-19, 125, 136, 145
Bhavani River, 176-77
Bhindranwale, 42
Brahminism, 151-52, 159, 166-68
Buddhism, 144, 159-60

casteism
    endogamy, 2, 6
    separate graveyard, 5
    rule of, 1-6, 23-32
    two-tumbler system, 3, 9
    See also Brahminism; Dalits;

Kallars; Mudaliars; Naidus; temple-entry; Vanniyars
Castro, Fidel, 20
change of names,
    retrieval of history, xi, xiii, xv, xxv-xxvi, 157-62
    Viduthalai Chiruthaigal, 157-64
Cauvery River issue, 175-78
chastity, 60
chaturvarna structure, 144
Chennai Central Prison police firing, 49, 56. *See also* police terrorism
Chennai Law College Hostel, 47-48, 51. *See also* police terrorism
Chidambaram Parliamentary elections, 35, 112-14. *See also* electoral violence
Christianity, 92, 144, 146, 160
cinema in TN, 93-96
Coimbatore riots, 55
Congress party, 90, 118, 135-37, 176. *See also* Sonia Gandhi
Constitution, 83, 91, 107, 117
Cuba, 22
custodial death, 48, 51
custodial rape, 48, 51-3

Dalits
    forced to drink urine, xi, 155-56
    forced to eat excrement, x, 119-22, 155-56
    unable to file nomination, 155
    See also casteism; Dr. Ambedkar; Viduthalai Chiruthaigal

devadasi system, 60-62, 88
Devaneya Pavanar, 158
double-vote system, 114
Dr. Ambedkar, 160
    and Buddhism, 45, 144
    and Dalits' Hindu identity, 160
    Panchasheel policy, 73
Dravida Munnetra Kazhagam
    (DMK), xv, xix, xxvi, 15-18,
    34, 40, 101-03, 110-11, 118,
    125-26, 132, 136-37, 176
Dravidian movement, 15-18, 94,
    153-54. *See also* ADMK;
    DMK; Periyar; Periyarism
drought in TN, 175-78
Durban conference, 6, 14, 19-22

Eelam. *See* Liberation Tigers
Election Commission, 64, 109-14
electoral violence, 12-13, 33-38,
    109-14. *See* also Election
    Commission; Chidambaram
    Parliamentary elections;
    Melavavu massacre, Panchayat
    constituencies
endogamy, 2, 6
Erampatti clash, 4, 9

Gandhi, M.K., 45
Gautama Buddha, 45
General Agreement on Tariffs and
    Trade (GATT), 141
globalization, 130, 140-41, 177
Gomathinayagam Commission, 53-
    54, 79
    Viduthalai Chiruthaigal, protest
    against, 79-80

Goondas Act, 11
Gopalakrishna Naidu, 77, 172-74.
    See also Venmani carnage
Guerilla Act, 132
Gujarat carnage, 92, 118, 153
Gundupatti, 10, 49. *See also* police
    terrorism
Harappan civilization, 166
Hindu Munnani, 55
Hinduism/Hindutva, 167-68
    and Dr. Ambedkar, 144
    co-option of Shaivism,
    Vaishnavism, 167
    definition of, 144
    imposition of identity, 160
    prohibition of religious conver-
    sion, 153, 155, 164
    Sanskrit as basis, 159, 168
    and Viduthalai Chiruthaigal's
    retaliation, 164
    worship of avatars, 166
human rights, 6, 41

Ilango Adigal, 59, 62. *See also*
    Kannagi; *Silappadhikaram*
Indian freedom struggle, 44-45
Indian National Congress. *See*
    Congress party
Indian Peace Keeping Force, 72. *See*
    also Liberation Tigers
Indira Gandhi, 137
Indus Valley civilization, 166
intercaste marriage, 2, 6
International Monetary Fund (IMF),
    141
Islam, 92, 118, 144, 146, 160

Index

Jainism, 144, 160
Jayalalitha, 16, 94, 97-100, 137, 151-55
judiciary. *See* Melavalavu massacre; Mohan/Gomathinayagam Commissions, Venmani carnage
K. A. P. Vishwanatham, 17
K. R. Narayanan, 105-08, 116-18
Kanchi Sankaracharaya, 106, 153, 155, 164
Kandadevi, 3, 7-8
Kannagi, 59-62
Kallars, 7, 14, 28-31, 36-37
kar seva, 81
Karnataka government, 176
Karunanidhi, 15-18, 94, 102-03. *See also* DMK
Kashmir, 123-24
Kaundampatti, 145, 155-56
Kerala government, 176
Kodiyankulam, 9-10, 48. *See also* Gomathinayagam Commission; police terrorism; Viduthalai Chiruthaigal
Koogaiyur, 160-64. *See also* temple-entry; Viduthalai Chiruthaigal
Koothirambakkam, 145, 160, 163. *See also* temple-entry
Kurinchankulam, 34, 37-38

legal terrorism, 39-42
Lenin, 72
liberalization, 130
Liberation Panthers. *See* Viduthalai Chiruthaigal
Liberation Tigers (LTTE), 123, 150
    Eelam Tamilians, 150
    government of, 147-50
    Heroes Day, 149
    ideological support, 124, 132
    Indian government, 72
    IPKF, 72
    liberation struggle, 150
    martyred heroes, 149
    rehabilitation of orphans, 150
    talks with Sinhalese government, 69-74
    Tamil language, 150
    training by India, 72
    Vanni Desam, 148

Maintenance of Internal Security Act (MISA), 39-41
majoritarianism, 89-92
Mandaikadu riots, 155-56
Manjolai estate workers, 49, 54, 78
    See also police terrorism, Mohan Commission
Manu Dharma, 46, 90, 92, 166
Maraimalai Adigal, 158
Marumalarchi Dravida Munnetra Kazhagam (MDMK), 40, 118, 132
Meenakshipuram, 156
Melavalavu massacre, 24-26, 30-31, 33-34
    memorial, 25
    judiciary, 76-77, 79-80
    accused, 79-80
    victims, list of, 25
    Viduthalai Chiruthaigal, role of, 25-30
M. G. Ramachandran, 15-18, 94, 158. *See also* ADMK

minorities, 89-92, 154
Mohan Commission, 54-55, 78
Mudaliars, 37
Mullai Periyar dam, 177
Musharraf, 135-37
Mustafa Kamal Pasha, 162

Naayanmar, 46
Nadu Kattamaippu, 26-27, 31-32, 76-77
Nagar Palika Acts, 65, 67-68
Naidus, 37, 57, 174
Nalayini, 60-62
Namakkal Kavignar, 70
National Democratic Alliance (NDA), 110, 125
national integration, 176
Nedunchezian V.R., 94
Nilgiri tea estate workers,129-30

Ogalur, 4, 10-12. *See also* police terrorism
Osama Bin Laden, 20, 42

P. C. Alexander, 116
Pakistan, 124
Palestinian problem, 19-21
Panchama, 167
Panchsheel Policy, 73
panchayat (general) constituencies
    Marukalampatti, 14, 35
    Sankaralingapuram, 56-58
    Sittampatti, 35
    Veliyambaakam, 35
panchayat (reserved) constituencies, 64-65, 122
    Keeripatti, 16, 23-24, 27-30, 36

Kottachiyendal, 28, 30
Melavalavu, 24-25, 30-31
Nattarmangalam,23, 29-30, 36
Pappapatti, 16, 23-24, 27-30, 36
Panchayati Raj Acts, 65, 67-8
Parithimar Kalaignar, 158
Pattali Makkal Katchi (PMK), 40, 99, 110, 112-14, 132
Pazha Nedumaran, 132
Periyar, xix-xx, 46, 65, 151-55. *See also* DMK, ADMK
Periyarism, 151-53
Peruncithiranar, 158
Piramalai Kallars. *See* Kallars
police terrorism
    Chennai Central Prison, 49, 56
    Chennai law college students, 47-48, 51
    Coimbatore riots, 49
    custodial deaths, 48, 51
    custodial rapes, 48, 51-53
    Gundupatti, 4, 10, 49
    Kodiyankulam, 4, 9-10, 48
    Manjolai estate workers, 49, 54-55
    Ogalur, 4, 10-12
    Sankaralingapuram, 56-58
    Vandavasi, 4, 12-13
    Veerappan-hunt, STF atrocities, 49, 56
Prabhakaran, 71, 97-100. *See also* LTTE
Prevention of Terrorist Activities Act (POTA), 39-42, 89-90, 123-24, 131-34, 136
privatization, 85-88, 127-30
    anti-social justice, 141

Kolar gold mines, 128
Neyveli Lignite Corporation, 85
Salem Steel Plant, 85, 128, 142
TN Transport Corporation, 86
Unit Trust of India, 139-42
Prohibition of Forcible Religious Conversion, 144-45, 153, 155-56, 161, 164
Puliyangudi murders, 5, 13-4, 34
Puthiya Tamizhagam, 7, 54

R. Nallakannu, 41
Raja Raja Cholan, 60-62, 88
Rajagopalachari, C., 17, 153
Rajinikanth, 95-96
Rajiv Gandhi, 65, 67-68, 71-72, 97-100, 123-24
Ram Janmabhoomi, 82
Ranil Wickremesinghe, 70. *See also* Sinhalese government; LTTE
Rashtriya Swayamsevak Sangh (RSS), 81, 91, 156
religious conversion,
  ban on, 156
  Dr. Ambedkar on, 144
  Koothirambakkam, 163
  Meenakshipuram, 156
  prohibition of, 144-45, 153, 155-56, 161, 164
  threat of, 163
  Venugopal Commission, 156
reservation, 75-6, 107
Rowlatt Acts, 42

saffronization, 43-6
Sanatana Dharma, 45
Sangh Parivar, 55, 81
Sankaralingapuram police atrocity, 50, 56-58. *See also* police terrorism
Sanskrit, 159
Scheduled Caste Federation, 90
Senguttuvan, 61-62
separate electorate, 114
Saivism, 82, 146, 168
shudra, 160, 167
Silappadhikaram, 59, 62. *See also* Kannagi
Sinhalese army, 147-49
Sinhalese government, 69-73, 147-49
Siruvatchi temple-entry, 26-27, 32
small gods, 166-67
Sonia Gandhi, 108, 135-38
Soviet Union, 72
starvation deaths, 127-130, 175
state terrorism, 22, 47-58
Suba Veerapandian, 132
Subramania Bharati, 70, 81
superpower terrorism, 22

Taliban government, 21
Tamil
  change of names, 157-63
  Eelam. *See* LTTE
  identity, 166, 177-78
  language, 150, 158
  nationalism, 131-34, 176-78
  struggle against Aryanism, 158
  Viduthalai Chiruthaigal, 157-63
  worship in, 165-8

Tamil Desiya Iyakkam, 132
Tamil Nadu Legislative Assembly, 101-04

temple-entry
   Viduthalai Chiruthaigal agitations for entry, 8, 155
   Azhagapuram, 3
   Kandadevi, 3
   Koogaiyur, 155
   Koothirambakkam, 14, 155
   Kurinchankulam, 34, 37-38
   Siruvatchi, 26-27
   Unchanai, 34, 36-37
Terrorist and Disruptive Activities (Prevention) Act (TADA), 39-42
Thamarabharani tragedy, 49, 54. *See also* police terrorism; Mohan Commission
Thamil Selvan, 71. *See also* LTTE
Thevars. *See* Kallars
Thinniyam atrocity, 119-22, 145-46, 155
   Viduthalai Chiruthaigal meeting on, 121-22
Thirumaavalavan. *See* Viduthalai Chiruthaigal
Thiruvalluvar, 65, 67
two-tumbler system, 3, 9

Unchanai, 34, 36-37
Uniform Civil Code, 91
Uttarakosamangai, 156

Vaiko, 124-26
Vaishnavism, 82, 146, 168
Vandavasi, 12
Vanniyars, 6, 8, 12-13, 37, 112, 163
Varnashrama Dharma, 166, 168

Veeran Sundaralingam, 65, 67
Veerappan hunt, 50
Venmani carnage, 7, 34, 169-74
   accused, aquittal of, 77, 174
   Gopalakrishna Naidu, 77, 172-74
   Marxists' role, 172-73
   memorial, 169-74
   and Viduthalai Chiruthaigal, 171-74
Venugopal Commission, 153-56
Viduthalai Chiruthaigal
   Anti-POTA front, 41
   Azhagapuram temple-entry, 8
   change of names, 157-64
   Chidambaram Parliamentary elections, 112-14
   Cuddalore district, 11, 13-14
   election boycott, 66
   and Gomathinayagam Commission, 79-80
   Goondas Act, 11
   Koogaiyur, 160-64
   K. R. Narayanan re-election, 108
   Law College students, 48
   Marukalampatti meeting, 35
   Melavalavu massacre, 14, 23, 25, 76, 79-80
   Ogalur, 10-12
   Panchayat constituencies,
      general 14, 35, 56-58
      reserved, 16, 23-31, 64-65, 122
   and Prohibition of Forcible Religious Conversion Act; 161
   Puliyangudi murders, 4-5, 13
   retaliation against Hindutva, 164

Sankaralingapuram, 50-51, 56-58
Thinniyam, 120-22
Vandavasi, 12
Venmani memorial, 169-73
worship in Tamil, 167
Vietnam, 22
Villupuram murders, 34, 37
Vishwa Hindu Parishad, 81

weavers' plight in TN, 127-30
World Bank, 141
World Conference Against Racism (WCAR), 14, 19-22
World Trade Center, 21
World Trade Organization, 141

Yasser Arafat, 21